Collins Wide World Encyclopedias

The Age of Machines

Compiled and edited by Kenneth Bailey

Collins

Glasgow and London

Written by David Roberts
Designed by Richard Hook

Illustrated by Fred Anderson, C. J. Ashford, Ronald Embleton, Richard Hook, Angus McBride, Peter North, Richard Sherrington, George Thompson

First published in this edition 1977
Published by William Collins Sons and Company Limited, Glasgow and London

© 1974, 1977 William Collins Sons and Company Limited
Printed in Great Britain
ISBN 0 00 106303 0

Contents

- **6 The Industrial Revolution**
  World Trade Centre
  Continental Europe
- **8 Cottage and Country**
  Farming Methods—Animals
  Breeding—Reaping Machines
  Canal-building—Road-building
  Bridges—Harbours and
  Lighthouses
- **12 Factory and Town**
  Spinning Machines—Power
  Looms—Continental Pottery
  English Bone China—Glass-making
  Industrial Glass—Precision Tools
  Machine Tools—Standards of
  Accuracy
- **18 Mining and Metals**
  Coal Hauling—Mining Safety
- **20 Modern Chemistry**
  Experiments with Air—Lavoisier's
  Experiments
- **22 The First Balloonists**
  Oxygen and Hydrogen—First
  Manned Ascent—Ballooning
  Craze
- **24 The Steam Engine**
  The Miner's Friend—Newcomen's
  Engines—James Watt
  High-pressure Steam
- **28 Industrial Progress**
  Transport
  Signalling Systems—Roads and
  Waterways—Bridge-building
  Tunnelling
- **Engineering**
  Textile Factories—Machine-tool
  Industry—Precision Tools
- **The Chemical Industry**
  Acid Production—Synthetic Dyes
  Explosives
- **Rubber**
  Sheet Rubber—The Macintosh
- **Coal-gas and Oil**
  Large-scale Lighting—Heating and
  Cooking—Petroleum Products
  Oil Drilling
- **Steel**
  The Bessemer Process—Open-
  hearth Furnaces—Rolling Mills
  Steel Alloys
- **40 The Specialist Scientists**
  The Structure of the Atom
  Dalton's Atomic Theory
  Chemical Symbols—Avogadro's
  Law—X-Rays—A Model of the
  Atom—Radium—Radioactivity
- **Theories of Light**
  Newton's Rings
- **Energy**
  Transformation of Energy
  Thermodynamics—$E = mc^2$
- **Magnetism and Electricity**
  Galvani and Volta—Magnetic
  Fields—The First Generator
- **Organic Chemistry**
  Organic Compounds
  Combination of Atoms
  Synthetic Materials
- **Germs and Disease**
  Louis Pasteur—Antiseptics
- **52 A New Age of Invention**
  Steam Carriages—Steamships
  Steam Turbines
- **Electricity**
  Electric Generators—Electric
  Railways—Incandescent Lamps
- **The Telegraph, Telephone and Radio**
  The Phonograph—Radio Signals
- **Internal Combustion**
  Daimler and Benz—The Bicycle
- **Powered Flight**
  Man-carrying Gliders—Powered
  Flight—Aeroplane Design

The Industrial Revolution

At the beginning of the 18th century, England must have seemed an unlikely place for a sudden burst of technological progress. Most of the population lived in rural communities, engaged in agriculture and cottage crafts. Technological know-how was largely imported from continental Europe. Mining engineers from Germany opened up the Cumberland copper mines. Canal builders from Holland drained the fenlands of East Anglia. French civil engineers advised on the establishment of the new turnpike roads. In the smelting of iron, England was behind even Russia. Sweden was then Europe's leading ironmaker both in quantity and quality. Yet what has been described as the most fundamental revolution in man's progress began in the north and midlands of England, in the lowlands of Scotland and in South Wales.

There were many reasons for this. England was a haven of religious freedom which attracted continental refugees, such as the Huguenots, who brought their technical skills with them. England had a population a third or even a quarter of France's, so there was a stimulus towards the invention of labour-saving devices. Particularly, this made farming in Britain highly efficient and released workers for the new industries. There was a much less rigid class system in Britain than elsewhere. Workers could advance by their own efforts to bring new vigour to a strong middle class. Landowners were ready to exploit their mineral resources and to invest in industry. Mill owners could buy country estates and were accepted into the highest society.

World Trade Centre

Geographically, Britain was well-placed to become a centre of world trade. Her long coastline provided ample ports, and navigable rivers were never far from the new factories. After 1745, new roads were constructed along which armies could be marched to deal with the aftermath of the Jacobite risings. Throughout the Industrial Revolution, Britain fought her wars abroad with professional soldiers. At home, industry was left at peace to get on with the job of creating wealth and to supply those armies and the navy for a programme of colonial expansion which itself created new markets for industrial products.

The English Revolution, as it has been called, began with improvements in agriculture and textile machinery. Dwindling supplies of home-grown timber stimulated coal-mining. Together with new puddling methods, the abundant deposits of coal and iron ore found close together created a rapid increase in the production of pig-iron. The power of wind, water and sheer muscle was slowly replaced by steam. New machinery that needed more power to operate it was assembled in factories. Instead of the work being distributed among the cottagers, workers were brought to the industrial centres where new towns mushroomed.

Continental Europe

All the new technology was available to the rest of Europe, but it was slow to take advantage of it. There was less mobility among the workers. There was serfdom in France until its own revolution of 1789, as well as in Germany, Austria and Russia well into the 19th century. Landowners were concerned only with agriculture, and a weak middle class was reluctant to invest in anything new. Despots like Frederick II of Prussia were obsessed with nationalised monopoly industries which have always stifled initiative. Powerful bureaucracies and trades guilds administered rules that restricted enterprise. National banks were conservative in their attitudes to new industry, whereas private banks in Britain had no difficulty in finding depositors and were eager for profitable investments. Wars that ravaged Europe upset trade and wasted both wealth and manpower.

It was inevitable that such rapid industrial expansion created new pressures. There were times of depression and unemployment. Workers were exploited by unscrupulous employers. Overcrowding undermined health. Factory chimneys polluted the atmosphere, and industrial waste destroyed the environment. Workers had to fight for their rights, for a fair share of the national cake, but at least there was a cake worth sharing.

From a basis of coal, iron and steam-power, the Industrial Revolution moved on to steel, electricity and the internal combustion engine. By that time, continental Europe and North America were catching up with Britain. Much of their early industrialisation had been started by British technicians and British-made machinery. Now others began to race ahead on their own initiative. As it had in Britain, a shortage of labour in America stimulated invention. Immigration from Europe, during the various periods of depression there, provided both a demand for consumer goods and a means of meeting it. In Europe, the spread of railways solved internal transport problems, and banking systems became more flexible. Innovations began to appear simultaneously in different countries. After 1850, it is often difficult to tell who invented what.

At the beginning of the Industrial Revolution, many of the inventors and innovators were artisans: spinners and weavers, blacksmiths and ironmongers, millwrights and wheelwrights. It was not long before the educated scientist became involved. For the first time, science and technology began to march hand in hand with the ambition to benefit the whole of society. This was to lead to the scientific research, backed by immense resources, that is such a feature of our own country.

For centuries coal mining in Britain was a small-scale industry, but increasing shortage of timber, which had provided charcoal for working iron, led in 1709 to the refinement by Abraham Darby of smelting pig iron with coke. From then coal mining was developed and Britain's supplies of both it and iron ore assured her lead in the Industrial Revolution.

Cottage and Country

Thomas Coke (1752–1842) improved crops and animal breeding methods on his estate.

An early 18th-century English village was an almost self-contained industrial complex. The corn-mill was its only custom-built structure to house large machinery, powered by wind or water. The blacksmith was the only engineer. The cottages were at the same time homes and mini-factories, where the spinning-wheel stood by the fireplace and the weaving-loom often took up more space than the family. Both machines had changed little since medieval times. In the early 16th century, a treadle had been added to the spinning-wheel to turn it with the foot by means of connecting rod and crank. This increased its output, but it still required between three and five spinners to supply one weaver.

In 1733, John Kay, a Lancashire weaver working in Colchester, patented his flying shuttle. It was rather like a toy boat on wheels that ran along a batten and carried the weft to and fro between the warp threads. It was operated by a cord attached to leather drivers running along metal rods. It enabled the weaver to drive the shuttle with one hand across a piece of cloth much wider than the span of his arms. One weaver could thus do the work of two, which intensified the search for a spinning machine to keep pace with him. The flying shuttle opened the way to a power-loom though it was entirely hand-operated at first. It also allowed the weaver to sit comfortably upright at his machine. Sadly Kay made little profit out of his invention which antagonised his fellow weavers and was pirated by unscrupulous employers.

Farming Methods

Meanwhile, improvements in farming methods were being pioneered by men like Jethro Tull, who, in 1701, invented a drill to plant seeds in rows. Horse-drawn and with a harrow attached behind, it covered the seeds it planted. Straight rows of growing corn made possible the use of a horse-drawn hoe which Tull introduced from France in 1714. He proved that continual tillage after sowing was particularly beneficial to root-crops, and he grew higher yields of wheat from less seed for thirteen successive years in unmanured fields.

The 18th century saw the end of the medieval three-field system which left a third of all agricultural land fallow each year. A new rotation of crops kept all the land under cultivation all the time. For this sort of intensive cultivation, landowners took to enclosing smaller fields with walls and hedges. There was a tendency to larger farms. Many smallholders and farmworkers were forced to leave the land altogether and seek employment in the growing towns. New crops were introduced to intersperse between grain crops. In England, these were particularly turnips, used as winter feed for animals, and clover, which fed the ground by fixing atmospheric nitrogen with the aid of bacteria in the roots, and also provided winter forage. The resulting increase in herds and flocks provided more manure for the further enrichment of the land. In 1747 a German chemist, A. S. Marggraf, discovered a beet with a rich sugar content. By 1840, there were 58 sugar-beet factories in France alone. They came much later to Britain who had ready access to the sugar-cane of the Caribbean.

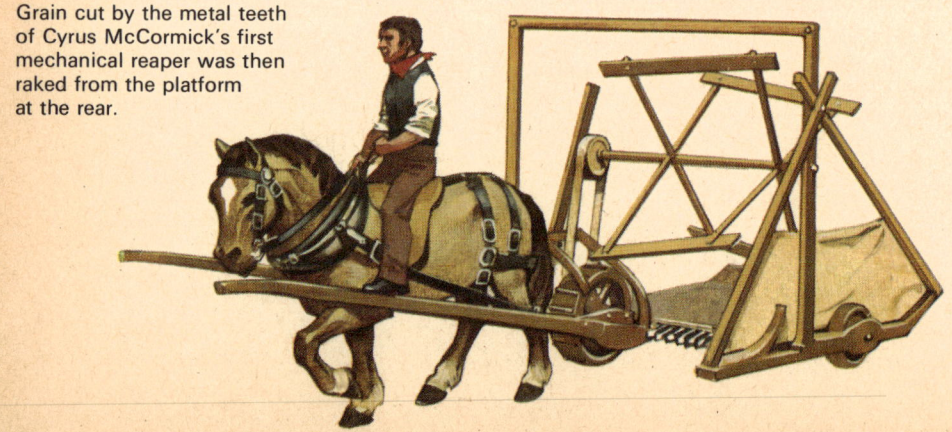

Grain cut by the metal teeth of Cyrus McCormick's first mechanical reaper was then raked from the platform at the rear.

The seed drill devised by Jethro Tull (1674–1741) was an efficient method of sowing and covering seeds in one operation.

The flying shuttle invented by John Kay (1704–64) was so distrusted by weavers that he was mobbed and forced to leave England.

Animal Breeding

In most of this, Holland and Flanders, forced by lack of space to introduce mixed farming in compact areas, provided the pioneers. Once the enclosure of fields had made it possible, however, British farmers began to lead the way in animal breeding. Robert Bakewell of Dishley created his Leicester sheep by selecting a stock to develop the most desirable points. They were small animals, but provided the maximum weight of the most valuable joints. In Spain, the merino sheep was developed for its wool and its secret jealously guarded. Nevertheless, it spread into Western Europe. George III of Britain had his own flock, though the efforts of most British breeders were directed towards meat production.

Bakewell also bred the Midland black horse, very powerful in relation to its size. It became a popular coach and dray horse. He was less successful with cattle than Charles Colling of Ketton in Yorkshire who developed the Durham shorthorn. Ayrshire cattle in Scotland were also improved through importations from Holland. So much did beef and mutton become part of the regular diet of the British and Dutch that they were regarded as gluttons by other Europeans. In England, improvements were publicised and spread by men like Thomas Coke of Holkham in Norfolk, local member of Parliament for 55 years and first Earl of Leicester. Coke and men like the Duke of Bedford and Lavoisier in France created model farms to conduct their experiments. The ancient practice of covering a light soil with clay containing limestone, called marling, was revived. From Holland came the use of organic waste from industry: from soap-boiling and tailoring; even scraps of horn from the handle-makers in the cutlery trade were used as fertiliser.

There was a whole series of inventions to aid the farmer. The small Dutch plough with its curved mouldboard partly covered in iron plate was improved in Britain by Robert Ransome of Ipswich who designed the all-iron plough. In 1789, he produced a cast-iron share in which the under surface was cooled more quickly than the upper so that, as the two surfaces wore unevenly, the plough sharpened itself. A few years later, his iron plough was designed with easily replaced, standard parts. The flail was still the universal instrument for separating grain from husks and straw until Andrew Meikle, a Scots millwright, produced in 1784 the first machine. It consisted of a drum rotating close to a curved shield so that the corn fed between the two had its husks rubbed off. At first it was powered by horses. In 1842, the steam-driven threshing machine appeared. By then, a winnowing machine to separate grain and chaff had been invented. A handle rotated a fan and agitated sieves in a box through which the grain passed. With a steam locomotive to drag thresher and winnower combined through the countryside and to operate them under contract with the farmers, this bit of farming automation became a common sight at harvest time.

Reaping Machines

Cutting corn was the job which employed most labour on an arable farm. Yet the designs for reaping machines which began to appear in Britain and America from 1780 onwards came to nothing until the American Cyrus McCormick patented his famous invention in 1834. A few years later, Americans were mowing

19th-century steam-powered ploughing: a cable running between two tractors pulled a double-ended plough from side to side of a field.

their hay with a machine which had a flexible cutter to compensate for uneven ground. Except for the thresher, most new machines were horse-operated. Attempts were made to introduce steam-ploughing whereby a stationary engine hauled the plough on the end of a cable. It was limited to suitable terrain and its high capital cost to the small farmer made it little more than a curiosity.

Advancements in farming technology and the manufacture of machinery for export kept Britain in the lead until the American Civil War began the rapid industrialisation of the United States. The war stimulated an increase in land use. Three successive years of bad harvests made Britain dependent on American imports. The New World rapidly overtook Europe in grain and meat production, and in the development of new machinery such as the first combine harvester, which cut and processed into sacks of grain twelve hectares (30 acres) of a standard crop in a single day. Between 1860 and 1900, over 160 million hectares (400 million acres) of land in the United States alone were newly brought under cultivation. This is an area ten times the total land mass of England and Wales. North America had become the granary of the world.

Canal-building

While the enclosure of fields and the new farming methods in 18th-century Britain were changing the face of her countryside, so were the civil engineers who set out to solve her transport problems. Among the first of these was James Brindley who began his career in 1733 at the age of seventeen as a repairer of millwheels. He worked out methods to improve the grinding of flints for the growing pottery industry. Travelling about in the course of his work, he began to survey England's waterways. The Duke of Bridgewater asked him to build a canal from the coal-mines on the duke's estate at Worsley in Lancashire to the growing town of Manchester 9·6 kilometres (6 miles) away. The finished canal was a remarkable engineering achievement including the first canal aqueduct to carry it at treetop height across the River Irwell.

Brindley went on to connect Manchester and Liverpool by water, and altogether laid out 640 kilometres (400 miles) of canal in different parts of the country. He was in many ways typical of the new generation of practical men who did so much to give Britain its industrial lead. He had very little conventional schooling. The men who dug canals were called navigators. It was because Brindley could not spell the word that the English for a labourer became navvy. Yet this untutored man worked out his own method of kneading clay to provide a waterproof bed for canal aqueducts. In 1805, the largest canal aqueduct ever built had an iron trough carrying the Ellesmere canal for a distance of 304 metres (1,000 feet) at a height of over 30 metres (100 feet) above the river Dee. It was engineered by Thomas Telford, another of the great Scottish canal-builders. By then, he had begun work on the Caledonian Canal in Scotland, the last major work before the railways began to take over.

Road-building

In road-building, the European leaders were the French, who had been the greatest canal-builders of the previous

James Brindley (1716–72), a poorly educated millwright who became a brilliant engineer.

Coping with the difficulties of canal building accelerated the development of civil engineering. The finance needed was raised by selling shares in specially created companies for every canal system, each with its seal.

To propel barges under bridges with no towpath they were 'legged' by two men who pushed against the walls on either side.

Henry Winstanley built the first Eddystone lighthouse whose wooden structure was washed away in 1703.

century. In a country controlled by all-powerful rulers, a national network of state-controlled highways was comparatively easy to establish. In 1720, a civil service was set up to look after roads and bridges. By the middle of the century, there was a training school for engineers in Paris. In 1776, France had built 40,000 kilometres (25,000) miles of state highways using the notorious *corvée* system of unpaid forced labour.

P. M. J. Trésaguet was the great 18th-century French road engineer. He invented a three-layer system in which a trench was dug and stones laid in the bottom on edge, hammered to form the contour of the final cambered surface. Two layers of smaller stones were then spread on top, the last of these, 7·5 cm. (3 inches) thick, composed of stones no bigger than a walnut. In Britain Thomas Telford, originally a stonemason, broadly followed Trésaguet's system, except that he started with a masonry pavement of large stones set on their broadest edge and the protuberances knocked off and used to fill intervening spaces. The two top layers of smaller stones were added in stages so that normal traffic could be used to impact the first layer before the second was added.

Bridges

France also had the first great bridge-builder, J. R. Perronet. He taught his engineers to flatten their arches to provide a gentle gradient for wheeled vehicles and to reduce the thickness of the piers. The temporary wooden centres used to support the arches as they were built were made of bolted pieces. When the bolts were removed, the whole temporary structure could be made to collapse into the river by pulling on ropes.

England had the first cast-iron bridge, built in 1779 across the river Severn by Abraham Darby of Coalbrookdale, third-generation owner of the famous ironworks there. Its main ribs were cast in sand-moulds with molten iron straight from the furnace. The bridge's parts were hoisted into position and held together by wedges without a single bolt or rivet. Though the masonry approaches have been repaired many times, the iron structure has stood the test of time and is still used by pedestrians today. America saw the first suspension bridge, built in 1800 in Pennsylvania by James Finley. It consisted of a deck hung on vertical rods from iron chains.

Harbours and Lighthouses

Men like Telford, laying new routes to speed the transportation of consumer goods, were not only road and bridge engineers, but also became involved in the improvement of harbours to which, on an island like Britain, the roads inevitably led. The Dutch, as might be expected, were the pioneers in the design of dredging equipment. About 1750, they invented the chain dredger which brought up the waste in buckets. With the later addition of steam-power, this became the system still essentially in use today.

In England, John Smeaton pioneered the technique of letting water do the work. In 1774, he began work on the entirely artificial harbour at Ramsgate in Kent. He enclosed an inner basin with six sluices from which water could be released at low tide. By sinking a barge in its path, the rushing water was made to gouge a way through the sand and deposit large quantities well beyond the harbour entrance. It was Smeaton who also designed the first of the great masonry lighthouse towers which are a feature of European coasts even today. Smeaton's new design was for the Eddystone rock which had had two previous lighthouses, mainly wooden structures.

By controlling the flow of water, sluice gates raised or lowered vessels to the next stretch of canal.

Factory and Town

The textile industry is the one usually chosen to illustrate the technological developments that gave rise to the Industrial Revolution. At first, the new technology was confined almost entirely to Britain. The appearance of the large textile factory was the first visible sign of it. A maritime nation, Britain's towns and cities were all on the coast or a river estuary. These were the centres of commerce, both for coastal shipping and international trade. It was not in such places that the factories first appeared. They were built in the villages where the textile crafts were practised. Here, labour (robbed since the enclosures of a livelihood from the land) was available, as was water-power from the rivers and streams. In time, these factory villages developed into the inland towns and cities of today.

Where the cottage industry had traditionally processed wool and linen-flax, the new material was cotton, imported in its raw state from the West Indies and the Middle East. It was this cheap raw material, available in large quantities, that stimulated the sudden spate of inventions. Cotton fibre had an elasticity that makes it easier than other fibres to spin by mechanical means. The old spinning-wheel was the bottleneck to any increase of output by the weaver. It was therefore the invention of spinning machines, particularly for cotton thread, that began the factory system.

Richard Arkwright was knighted in 1786.

Spinning Machines

The famous name in cotton-spinning is that of Lancashire-born Richard Arkwright (1732–92), who began his working life as a barber. His spinning machine may not have been his own invention. His patent rights in it were later taken from him in a court action. At the top it had four wooden bobbins set horizontally on which the raw cotton, cleaned and carded (i.e. combed out) was twisted. From these, a thread was drawn through two pairs of rollers, the second turning faster than the first so that the cotton was drawn out into a longer and finer thread to be wound on to lower bobbins. About the same time, in the 1760s, a carpenter and weaver called James Hargreaves invented his spinning-jenny. With this, the raw cotton was placed on bobbins at the bottom of the frame and drawn out by a bar that moved to and fro across the top. The spun cotton was taken up on spindles at the opposite end. About 1779, Samuel Crompton, a farmer who devoted more time to textiles than he did to his own land, invented the spinning-mule, a combination of the other two machines, incorporating both rollers and a moving bar.

At first, these machines were designed to be operated by hand, by water-power or by horses. In 1785, a steam engine was built to supply

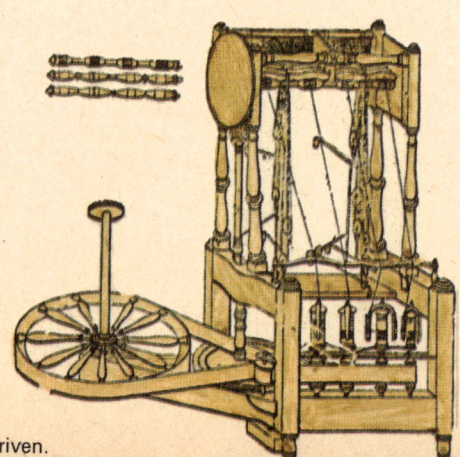

Arkwright's spinning frame was water-driven.

power to a spinning factory at Popplewick in Nottinghamshire. Its success led to a slow but continuous growth of steam-power for all the operations in textile production. Most of this development led to more and more factories being built. But steam-power came even to the cottage industry, as at Coventry where rows of silk-weavers' cottages each had their steam engines built behind them. This is not to say that hand-looms did not continue far into the 19th century. But the new pattern of life for most workers was fixed. Small factory towns began to mushroom wherever there was coal or water-power readily available.

Power Looms

Speeding up spinning reversed the old bottleneck situation. Now weavers could no longer keep pace with the supply of thread or the demand for cheap cotton fabrics. A Leicestershire parson, Edmund Cartwright, became aware of the problem on a visit to the cotton-spinning valley of the Derwent in Derbyshire during the summer of 1784. He met some men from Manchester who were discussing the likely spread of spinning-mills when Arkwright's patents ran out. Cartwright had the sort of mind that delights in problems. He was used to doctoring his parishioners as well as preaching to them. Within three years, he had invented a power-loom and set up a factory of his own in Doncaster.

It would be nice to say that he prospered from his ingenuity. His machine had drawbacks, however, and his factory was forced to close within half a dozen years. A Manchester firm who took up the idea had their factory burned down by irate weavers afraid for their livelihood. Cartwright had shown the way though, and other inventors solved the problems of his machine. By 1809, there were more than 2,000 power-looms in Britain and Cartwright was awarded £10,000 by a grateful government. The march of progress could not be stayed.

In the years that followed, machines powered by water or steam were created for every operation in the textile industry. Men like Richard Roberts set up in business as machine-makers. Roberts spent £12,000 perfecting a fully self-acting spinning machine. It was Roberts who built the standard power-loom of his day, based on a system invented by William Horrocks of Stockport. A method was devised whereby cam-wheels operated levers to raise different sets of warp

The interior of a 19th-century textile factory.

Samuel Crompton's spinning-mule was the first to produce a fine thread.

Edmund Cartwright (1743–1823)

The loom invented by Jacquard (1752–1834) was the first machine to weave in patterns.

threads for weaving fancy fabrics. Soon, however, a French silk-weaving loom developed in 1801 by J. M. Jacquard at the command of Napoleon was adapted to the weaving of fancy worsteds. It had a punched-card system for lifting needles which controlled the threads to be raised. It was essentially the system still used today. Europe had followed Britain's lead in textiles, but was now beginning to make its own way.

Continental Pottery

In pottery, continental Europe was already ahead of Britain at the beginning of the Industrial Revolution. England's contribution from the beginning of the 18th century was the development of cheap, factory-produced soft-paste porcelain, particularly in the area of Staffordshire known ever since as the Potteries. China began to replace the use of vessels made from wood, leather and metals such as pewter. It was easier to clean and similar to cotton in improving the nation's health and opening up a vast new market among ordinary people. Continental pottery was much more of a luxury trade, centred on the production of finely-decorated, hard-paste porcelain in imitation of the high quality importations from China.

In 1710, J. F. Böttger, chemist to Augustus the Strong of Saxony, first found a process to rival the Chinese, whose secrets had been carefully kept since ancient times. He used powdered alabaster and marble with a particularly white china clay, using a new type of kiln giving temperatures as high as 1,400°C. Before, only soft-paste delftware had come anywhere near to the appearance of Chinese pottery, often directly copying its decoration. Böttger's discovery established the famous Dresden pottery at Meissen. His process was also kept secret until, in 1768, P. J. Macquer, chief chemist at the state-owned pottery of Sèvres in France, produced a hard-paste to rival Meissen. In the same year, a British chemist, William Cookworthy, made the same discovery. Two years later, he began manufacturing in Bristol from where his process spread to Hanley in the Potteries.

English Bone China

As well as at Delft, soft-paste porcelain was produced at Sèvres until the pottery there found out how to make the more highly prized hard-paste. England's contribution was in new ingredients such as soapstone (hydrated magnesium silicate) used in Worcester after 1752. In London, the pottery factories at Bow and Chelsea began using bone-ash as an ingredient. The idea came from Germany, but English bone-china quickly became famous throughout Europe. What first made the fortunes of the Potteries, however, was a development made by John Astbury about 1720. This involved mixing a white-burning clay with finely-powdered flint, the final product being known as stoneware. Canal-builder Brindley was involved in devising effective flint-mills. About 1750, double-firing was introduced, first at the so-called biscuit stage and then after dipping in a liquid glaze containing lead oxide. The flint lightened the colour of the final product and increased its hardness. Mills for grinding the flint were one of the earliest users of steam-power.

Staffordshire pottery was typical of many English innovations which together make up the beginnings of the Industrial Revolution. Cheap products in vast quantity were aimed at international mass markets. The leading name in this growing industry was Josiah Wedgwood, a potter's son who was himself throwing pots at the age of nine. Wedgwood improved the local cream stoneware, using no coloured decoration but adopting classical designs to shape his products. In 1762, Queen Charlotte accepted a set and this style of pottery became known as Queen's ware. Wedgwood was appointed royal potter. He employed John Flaxman to design white relief ornamentation on coloured backgrounds and revived the ancient use of moulds to speed production. With the invention of transfer printing of coloured patterns, the way was open to mass production with division of labour along a production line. The final improvement to bone-china came when the Spode family added felspar to the mixture at their factory in Stoke-on-Trent, creating the easily worked porcelain material still used today. An increasingly scientific approach developed with precise analysis of the raw materials, exact kiln temperatures and careful factory procedures.

Glass-making

In glass manufacture, an important scientific advance was made when John Dolland invented a lens which eliminated the rainbow effect of light refraction. He cemented a convex lens of crown glass to a concave lens of flint glass to produce achromatic lenses, patenting the process in 1758. This led to the large reflecting telescopes such as the twelve-metre (40-

18th-century porcelain. Top: a Wedgwood vase of 1786; a Sèvres plate of 1772. Centre: 'The Young Suppliant', a figure from the French pottery at Vincennes, 1752. Bottom: a tea-pot from St Petersburg; a Meissen piece 'The Allegro' dating from about 1740.

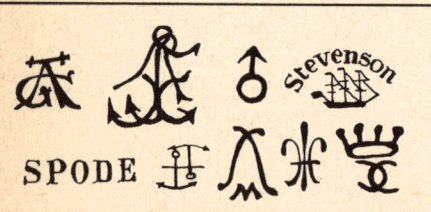

European 18th-century pottery marks.

foot) example built by William Herschel in 1789. The year before, P. L. Guinand of Switzerland had discovered that stirring molten flint glass with a fireclay stirrer distributed its heavy lead oxide content more evenly and produced a better optical glass. It also dispersed air bubbles in the mixture, improving light transmission. The secret of this process, developed in Munich in association with Joseph von Fraunhofer, was kept until both men died. Then it was purchased by the French glass-maker, Georges Bontemps, who brought it to England during the revolution of 1848 and formed a partnership with the firm of Chance Brothers.

It was in Germany and France that a new method of making sheet glass was first practised. A ball of glass, as much as eighteen kilograms (40 pounds) in weight, was blown into a globe and then rolled in a trench to give it a cylindrical shape. The two ends were cut off and the cylinder slit lengthways with a diamond-tipped tool. Reheated to soften it, the cylinder was then unrolled into a flat sheet. For better quality glass, the cylinder was opened out on a glass-covered stone, smoothed with a block of wood and hardened in a special kiln. The process was not introduced into Britain until 1832. Meanwhile, a plate-glass factory established in 1776 at Ravenhead near St Helens in Lancashire boasted a casting-hall with a floor area 118 by 45 metres (130 by 50 yards), one of the largest factory buildings of its time. As early as 1789, the new steam engines were used to power the grinding and polishing processes.

Industrial Glass
In these early years, Britain established a reputation for cutting and engraving the finest crystal glass and made several advances in colouring processes. These were confined to the luxury trade. The full industrialisation of glassware had to wait until 1887 when the first commercially-successful bottle-making machine came into use at Castleford in Yorkshire, to be improved in 1898 by M. J. Owens in America. Chance Brothers developed a semi-automatic process of producing plate-glass by pouring the molten material on to an inclined plate, passing it between rollers and then on to grinders and polishers. This depended for its mechanisation on the improved gas-fired furnaces recently developed by the German firm of Siemens. These eventually provided a continuous flow of molten glass. By then, as in the pottery industry, the chemical combination of the materials had been scientifically defined. Ernest Abbé, Otto Schott and Karl Zeiss joined forces in 1886 at the famous Jena glassworks in Germany to improve optical glass. By the end of the century, the company was producing about 80 different kinds of glass and had introduced 28 new elements into its composition.

The factory system did not just take the production of consumer goods away from the individual craftsman. To succeed, it had to make goods cheaper by producing them in greater quantity. The new work-force assembled in the factories was not made up entirely of skilled craftsmen. There were never enough of these available. As time went on, the speed of production required a precision of which even skilled hands were not always capable. New machines had not only to be invented, they had to be manufactured in sufficient numbers to meet the demand for them. It is not surprising, therefore, that this period

The 18th-century method of casting sheets of plate glass.

England's skill in engraving glass was developed in the late 17th century when a flint glass containing lead oxide was made. This was both brilliant and soft enough for cutting.

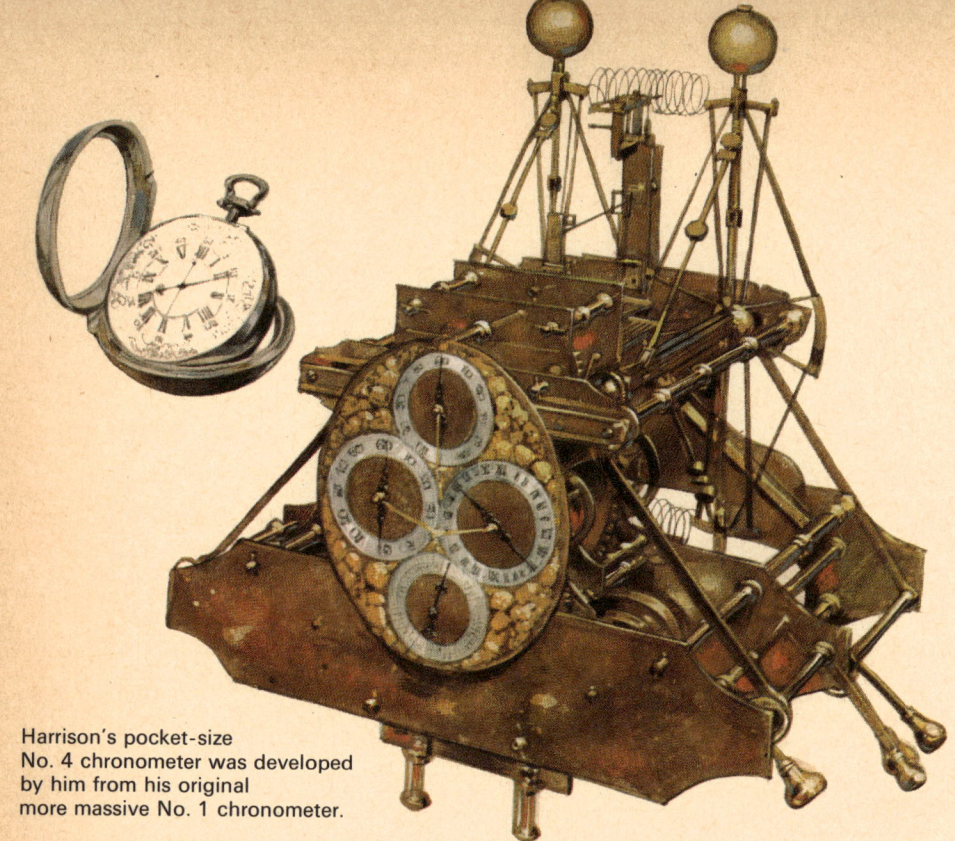

Harrison's pocket-size No. 4 chronometer was developed by him from his original more massive No. 1 chronometer.

saw the development of an entirely new machine-tool industry. The craftsman had often made his own tools. The factory worker was the operator of machine-tools that were themselves made in factories.

Precision Tools
It was the makers of clocks and scientific instruments who first found the need for precision tools. The French were the masters at producing automata, clockwork playthings that went through a sequence of beautifully flowing movements. They represent the beginning of modern automation. The British had a more practical turn of mind. In the early decades of the 18th century, clock-making progressed from a craft in the hands of a few skilled makers to a national industry that captured the European market. In 1759, John Harrison completed his famous chronometer No. 4. It won the £20,000 prize which had been offered by the Board of Longitude from as far back as 1714. This chronometer enabled seamen to estimate their longitude within an accuracy of half a degree.

Clock-making required accurate lathes that began to appear from 1700 onwards. In 1750, the Frenchman Antoine Thiout introduced a tool-holding carriage which moved the cutter across the workpiece. Jacques de Vaucanson invented an improved lathe and a drill working on the same principle. In 1770, an English instrument maker, Jesse Ramsden, devised the first satisfactory screw-cutting lathe with an accuracy sufficient for the screws used in measuring instruments like the micrometer. It was Ramsden, too, who produced the first dividing-engine for use on an industrial scale. In 1757, the sextant had come into use as an aid to navigation. Its graduated scale had to be marked off very accurately. Dividing-engines like Ramsden's speeded up the job. In France in the early part of the 19th century Henri Gambey was producing even more accurate instruments. His dividing-engine graduated a 2-metre circle at the Paris Observatory in 1840 which remained in use for 80 years. He even introduced remote control so that metal expansion from the body heat of the operator was avoided.

Machine Tools
The desire for accuracy was reflected in larger industrial machine-tools. In their manufacture a number of English engineers were the pioneers. In 1775, John Wilkinson set up his famous boring-mill in his father's ironworks in Denbighshire. A hollow boring-bar was supported in a bearing at one end and driven from a large wheel at the other. The cutter rotated with the bar and was moved along it by a rod within the bar. Originally designed for boring cannon, it was easily adapted to the production of accurate cylinders for steam engines, for which it had a monopoly for twenty years. Without it, the steam engine itself could never have reached an early state of efficiency, and its design remained much the same into the middle of the next century.

Another famous name in the machine-tool industry is that of Joseph Bramah, son of a Yorkshire farmer. Among other things, he invented a hydraulic press, a wood-planing machine, a machine for printing serial numbers on banknotes and a patent lock that remained unpicked for 67 years despite the standing offer of a 200-guinea prize. The American visitor who finally picked Bramah's lock took 51 hours spread over sixteen days. Bramah also built a spring-winding machine with a geared leading-screw which could be set to wind springs of predetermined pitch. From this, Bramah's foreman, Henry Maudslay, devised a screw-cutting machine. Finding that his ingenuity did nothing to raise his 30-shillings-a-week wage, Maudslay set up his own firm in 1797.

His first major order was for machine-tools for Portsmouth naval dockyard. Marc Brunel, a royalist refugee from the French navy, had designed machinery for manufacturing pulley-blocks. In 5½ years from 1802, Maudslay built 43 machines for sawing, boring, mortising and scoring three sizes of pulley-blocks. Driven by a 30 hp steam engine, these machines produced 130,000 blocks a year with ten unskilled men in place of the 110 skilled men employed before. It was another portent of the labour versus machinery controversy that has beset industry in the western world ever since.

Standards of Accuracy
Maudslay set a new standard of accuracy for all machine-tools, partly with his insistence on all-metal construction. He also trained the next generation of great machine-tool engineers, among them Richard Roberts who made the first metal-planing machine in 1817. A larger version was produced a few years later by Joseph Clement, another of Maudslay's employees. It became the main source of Clement's income, earning him as much as £20 a day, and remained for ten years the only machine of its kind capable of handling a workpiece 1·8 metres (6 feet square).

James Nasmyth was Maudslay's personal assistant until the latter's death, when he set up his own workshop. He invented several machines, but is particularly famous for his steam-hammer. Designed in 1839, it consisted of a hammer-head connected to the piston of an overhead cylinder. Steam admitted beneath this piston raised the hammer for each

'Fritz', a 19th-century German steam hammer for working steel.

stroke. Later, steam was also forced in above the piston to increase the power of the downward stroke. With this machine, iron girders and plates of a size never known before could be forged. Yet the great hammer could be controlled to descend with a force just sufficient to crack an egg. A version of Nasmyth's steam-hammer drove the piles for Robert Stephenson's Newcastle bridge at the rate of one blow per second instead of one every few minutes by previous methods.

Last of the these early pioneers was Joseph Whitworth who also worked for Maudslay for a short time. In 1833, he set up business as a maker and seller of machine-tools. This was a new idea, since all the other machine-tool engineers mentioned had been involved in using the machines they produced. At the Great Exhibition of 1851 in London, he had 23 exhibits of which one was a planing-machine with reversible tool-holder so that cuts could be made in both directions. He produced a measuring-machine accurate to ·0000025 centimetres (one-millionth of an inch) and worked towards standardisation of screw-threads, so that screws might become generally interchangeable.

Mining and Metals

Sir Humphry Davy (1778–1829) devised his safety lamp to show the presence of fire-damp. Before then canaries, more quick than men to react to the gas, were used to detect it.

Right: a Davy safety lamp. Centre: token money, like the coins minted by the ironmaster John Wilkinson of Bradley, was used to pay wages in the chronic absence of state coin. Bottom: the method of removing fire-damp, replaced by the Davy lamp.

In early 18th-century Britain, there was what could be described as a coal rush. Many landowners were involved. If coal was found even beneath the sweeping lawns and flower beds of a gentleman's estate, he had no compunction in ripping it all up to get at the black gold. When surface workings were exhausted, mines were sunk ever deeper.

The most common method of extraction in a deep mine was known as bord-and-pillar. Bords (an obsolete spelling of board) were the first excavations made at right angles to the seam, dividing the rest of the coal into pillars anything from 20 to 55 metres (22 to 60 yards) square. Slices about 5·5 metres (six yards) wide were cut from these. The roof was supported by timbers during the cutting and then allowed to collapse. In very deep mines, where the pressure was too great for the roof to be supported by timber, coal was removed in one go by the system known as longwall working. A wall of coal about 90 metres (100 yards) long was taken out and the roof above supported by stone piles as the cutting advanced.

Coal Hauling

Coal was hauled away from the face in wicker baskets loaded on to sledges. The baskets were then carried up the shaft by a series of ladders and landing stages, sometimes to a height of more than 30 metres (100 feet). While the men did the actual coal-cutting, their wives and children hauled away the coal. As distances became greater, pit ponies were introduced from about 1763. Towards the end of the century, trucks running on light rails were used, though more often than not women and children still did the hauling. Some galleries could be tunnelled with an upward slope so that loaded trucks could run to the shaft down an incline. Others had dips which increased the haulage difficulties, or were too low for a pony to stand upright. Steam-haulage was gradually introduced, even in level galleries, and power winding gear was used to raise coal and miners up the shaft.

Flooding and ventilation were ever-present problems. Again, steam-power was eventually used for pumping out water. Black-damp, air deficient in oxygen, was the main problem in shallow mines, but could be noticed quickly by the miner when his lamp

A French pit pony being lowered to its work in the mine.

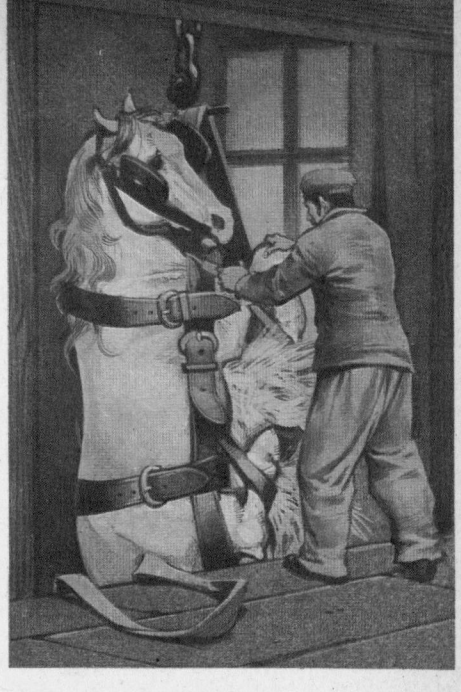

dimmed. The use of explosives to get at and move the coal often caused after-damp, the product of incomplete combustion after an explosion. Fire-damp, a mixture of air and methane gas released from the cut coal, was a third hazard. A fireman was employed to go ahead of his companions, wrapped in wet sacks and holding a naked flame on the end of a long pole to burn away the gas. A flint-and-steel mill, which emitted a stream of sparks bright enough to work by, gave warning of explosive gas when the sparks grew bigger and brighter. A number of safety lamps were devised, the most famous of which was designed by the scientist Sir Humphry Davy. The flame was contained within a metal gauze cylinder which carried away the heat before it could ignite any gas. A second gauze was later added to avoid the danger when the first gauze became red-hot, as it could in a strong draught. Davy's experiments in this field illustrate how, for the first time, pure science was beginning to be applied to the solution of practical problems.

Mining Safety

Every improvement in mining safety and technique was slow in coming. By 1900, twelve-year-old boys still went underground. Disastrous explosions continued to be a frequent occurrence. No satisfactory coal-conveyor was introduced until 1902. The early mechanical cutters, like circular saws, were driven by compressed air. Electric coal-cutters were a later innovation. Well into our own century, the coal-face worker had to lie or crouch in wet or unbearably hot conditions, hacking a deep groove close to floor level, then pull down the coal mass with pick, crowbar or hammered wedge. For some, human muscle was still the prime force.

A growing shortage of timber in Britain had stimulated the coal rush. The use of coal for the smelting of iron-ore was to bring together the two great raw materials of the Industrial Revolution. When brewers tried to dry their malt by coal fires, the taste of the beer was ruined. We know now that this was because of the presence of sulphur. In the 17th century, some Derbyshire brewers had the idea of charring the coal to make coke, which has most of its sulphur removed, just as wood is charred to make charcoal. The result was a famous beer. Similarly, smelting iron-ore with coal introduced impurities into the metal, making it brittle and difficult to work. In 1709, Abraham Darby, who had served his apprenticeship to a malt-mill manufacturer, experimented with coke-smelting of iron. He achieved a reasonable success with the production of pig iron, but did not advertise his process. In 1748, his son of the same name, by careful selection of ores with low phosphorus content, managed to produce coke-smelted cast iron. Later, the quality of the iron was improved by remelting in foundry furnaces where the iron was not in contact with the coal burnt in them.

Coke in a blast furnace burned less easily than charcoal. John Smeaton partly overcame this by introducing blowing cylinders powered by water to provide more air for complete combustion. John Wilkinson in 1776 started the use of a steam engine to provide the air blast. In 1784, Henry Cort established the puddling process which essentially involves the raking, separating, stirring and spreading of the melted ore within the furnace to give the air complete and rapid access to it. The Clyde Ironworks in Glasgow introduced, in 1829, the hot blast which produced three times as much iron with the same amount of fuel. The principal metal for the new industries was becoming cheap and plentiful.

Progress in the production of other metals was somewhat slower. Benjamin Huntsman of Doncaster, a clock and instrument maker, produced an improved steel. He heated bar iron and charcoal in special heat-resisting clay crucibles for five hours at a very high temperature. This crucible steel gradually became adopted by the cutlers of Sheffield where Huntsman moved to exploit his invention. But steel remained a costly, small-scale process.

One notable new use of metal was the invention in 1742 by Thomas Bolsover of Sheffield plate, at first for making buttons. Thin sheets of silver were soldered or fused on to either side of a thick sheet of copper. This sandwich was then rolled into a thin sheet. Cheaper than pure silver, its use spread for such articles as tea and coffee services and candlesticks, especially after a technique was introduced for soldering a silver wire to cover the edges where the copper was exposed.

Sheffield plate was a popular substitute for solid silver and after 1784 had its own hallmark. Left: Until about 1900, children were used to drag coal from the face.

By co-ordinating and extending the work of others, Lavoisier founded modern chemistry.

Modern Chemistry

The study of chemistry could not advance until the processes of combustion and chemical combination were understood. This understanding was the great scientific breakthrough of the 18th century. We owe it to the work of one of France's most eminent scientists, Antoine Laurent Lavoisier (1743–94). Yet his years of experiment discovered no new chemical substance and established few new chemical facts. What he did was to interpret the discoveries of others, to formulate a new theory of combustion, to explain the basic simplicity of chemical combination and to give a start to the modern naming of such combinations and the elements comprising them. It was the foundation on which the modern study of chemistry was to be built.

When Lavoisier was beginning his chemical experiments, scientists still believed in the phlogiston theory put forward in the previous century by Johann Joachim Becher and developed by his disciple Georg Ernst Stahl. The theory stated that when a substance burns it gives off fire stuff or phlogiston. Something like charcoal which leaves very little ash behind was considered to be almost pure phlogiston. Lavoisier burned phosphorus in a bottle to the neck of which was attached a bladder of air and showed that a sizeable proportion of the air was absorbed by the burning phosphorus. He did the same experiment with sulphur with similar results. This seemed to contradict the phlogiston theory which claimed that when phosphorus and sulphur burn, rather than absorbing anything, they emit phlogiston.

When metals like lead and tin are melted, they leave a dross on the surface called a calyx, the process called calcination. It was known that this calyx was heavier than the metal from which it was formed. Adherents of the phlogiston theory explained this by saying that phlogiston has levity rather than gravity, or that it possessed negative weight. Lavoisier, believing that the increase in weight came from the absorption of air, heated some lead in a sealed vessel until there was no further calcination. Weighing the vessel before and after this process, he found no change in the weight. When he unsealed the vessel, he heard an inrush of air. The weight of the vessel and its contents had then increased by an amount equal to the increase in the weight of the calyx. These experiments showed that the amount of air available is the critical factor in the extent to which calcination takes place. Only a part of the air, about a fifth, is absorbed. What was the peculiar nature of this one-fifth of the air?

The answer came from the experiments of an English Unitarian minister called Joseph Priestley (1732–1804), interested in the investigation of gases. Priestley devised an apparatus with a retort attached by a tube through a bath of mercury to a gas-collecting vessel. With the aid of a powerful burning-glass, he heated some red calyx of mercury (mercuric oxide, HgO). He found that the calyx changed into mercury and that a gas was given off. This new gas caused a candle flame to burn with astonishing vigour. He put a mouse in a quantity of the gas. In the same amount of air, the mouse would be expected to live about fifteen minutes. It lived for half an hour. Taken out, apparently dead, it revived in front of the fire. Priestley called his new gas dephlogisticated air because, as a supporter of combustion it must readily absorb phlogiston. We, of course, call it oxygen.

Experiments with Air
Lavoisier repeated Priestley's experiments. He heated mercury calyx with charcoal and collected the gas that was emitted. This gas extinguished a candle flame and killed animals placed in it in a few seconds. It was obviously the gas discovered in 1756 by the Scottish chemist, Joseph Black, and called fixed air (carbon dioxide, CO_2). Lavoisier next heated mercury calyx by itself. This time, the gas given off made a candle flame flare up brilliantly and supported the breathing of animals. It seemed to be particularly pure air. Lavoisier concluded that what combines with a substance when it is burned or calcinated is this pure air. Eventually, he showed that ordinary air consists of two gases, one that supports combustion and respiration (oxygen) and another that does neither (nitrogen).

He heated mercury in a vessel connected to the air in a bell jar standing in a bath of mercury. The heating continued until no more red calyx of mercury appeared. Then by heating the mercury calyx and the air in a number of ways, Lavoisier disproved the phlogiston theory. This stated that heating mercury in oxygen made it release its phlogiston into the oxygen. Lavoisier demonstrated that, on the contrary, all the oxygen present was absorbed to create the mercury calyx.

Another great British experimenter, the eccentric millionaire Henry Cavendish (1731–1810) had discovered another gas obtained from the action of acids on metals. It was highly inflammable, and he called it inflammable air which we now know as hydrogen. In 1781, Priestley ignited a mixture of inflammable air and about a fifth of the ordinary air was changed into a liquid. The liquid had no taste or smell and left no deposit when evaporated. It seemed to be, and indeed was, pure water. Lavoisier repeated these experiments and laid claim to the discovery. He had not, of course, discovered the composition of water. But he did realise, as Cavendish did not, that water could no longer be regarded as an element as it had been from ancient times. He had the genius to perceive that inflammable air and dephlogisticated air are the true elements, and that their chemical combination produces water. It was this momentous explanation that eventually led chemists to look for the elements combined in all substances that were not themselves elements. Modern chemistry was born.

Lavoisier's Experiments
Lavoisier went on to name the substances that had been discovered. Dephlogisticated air became oxygen and the calyx of a metal its oxide. Inflammable air became hydrogen. Pure charcoal was called carbon and its salts carbonates. The combination of sulphur and oxygen became sulphuric acid and its salts sulphates, and so on. Lavoisier, as a rich man, fell foul of the revolutionary leaders in his country and was brought to trial. In his defence it was claimed that, as a scientist, he had brought honour to France. The President of the court replied: 'The Republic has no need of men of science', and Lavoisier went to the guillotine.

Henry Cavendish reconstructed the Torsion Balance experiment to determine the earth's specific gravity. He measured the torsion, or twisting, caused to a thread suspending two small spheres attracted by two large spheres.

Priestley's sympathy for the French Revolution led in 1791 to the wrecking of his house by a mob. In 1794 he emigrated to the United States.

The First Balloonists

Francesco de Lana's 1670 design for an aerial ship. Most early designs for flying machines were based on the use of birdlike wings, and it was not until the possibilities of lighter-than-air gases were realised that practical designs were produced. The first successful balloon used heated air to provide lift.

It was the 18th-century interest in gases and the discoveries resulting from them that began the new and often dangerous pastime of ballooning. The balloonists themselves approached their problems in a spirit of scientific enquiry, prepared to risk their lives in practical experiment. The Montgolfier brothers, Joseph and Etienne, French papermakers, began it all.

Oxygen and Hydrogen

Their first hot-air balloon was not designed to carry passengers, though big enough to do so. Their aerostatic machine, as they called it, was made of cloth lined with paper. It was spherical with a circumference of 34 metres (110 feet). A wooden frame 4·6 metres (16 feet) square held it fixed at the bottom. Its capacity was about 625 cubic metres (22,000 cubic feet), so it displaced a volume of air weighing 898 kilograms (1,980 pounds). The weight of the hot air that filled it they estimated at 450 kilograms (990 pounds) and the weight of the fabric of the machine at 227 kilograms (500 pounds). It was the 221 kilograms (490 pounds) difference between the balloon's total weight and the weight of air it displaced which caused it to rise. Two men could lift the structure to fill it with hot air from a fire on the ground. But once filled, it took eight men to hold it down. It remained ten minutes in the air. The hot air soon escaped through the buttonholes of the buttons that held it together, was replaced by cold and heavier air, and it floated gently down. At last, on 5th June 1783, aeronautics became a practical possibility. In September, 1783, the brothers' fourth experiment included the first living passengers, a sheep and some pigeons carried in a basket suspended beneath the balloon.

First Manned Ascent

The following month, the first manned ascent was undertaken by the Marquis d'Arlandes and Pilâtre de Rozier. This time, the fire that provided the hot air was slung under the balloon itself and a supply of straw for fuel was carried with the two passengers. The 25 minute flight carried them nearly 9 kilometres (5½ miles) across Paris. They landed safely, though de Rozier had to crawl out from under the enveloping folds of the collapsed balloon.

Almost as soon as the hot-air balloon had achieved its first success, the hydrogen balloon appeared. This was the invention of the French scientist Professor Jacques Charles. His first experiment was launched on 27th August 1783 without passengers. His balloon landed in the village of Gonesse, where the local people were so terrified by its sudden appearance that they hacked it to pieces with their scythes and forks. Professor Charles was the real creator of the balloonists' art. He invented the valve to control the gas content, the car to carry passengers, the sand for ballast, the coating of caoutchouc (india-rubber) to make the balloon airtight and the practice of carrying a barometer to measure altitude. Nevertheless, he only ever made one trip in a balloon, during which his companion left him at the first landing, while the professor flew on alone, the first solo aviator in the world.

It was a Frenchman, too, who made the first parachute descent from a balloon, on 22nd October 1797. His name was André Garnerin. His parachute was attached to the small basket in which he stood, and all this was suspended beneath the balloon. At 610 metres (2,000 feet), he cut the cord which connected the parachute to the balloon. At first he fell swiftly, but then the air caught in the parachute, opened it out and brought him gently to earth. Garnerin was eventually killed experimenting with a parachute, but his pioneer efforts and considerable courage certainly helped to save many lives in later years.

Ballooning Craze

The craze for ballooning spread throughout Europe and to America. In 1785, Blanchard and Jefferies made the first crossing of the English Channel. Soon the military authorities were beginning to take an interest. A balloon was first used for military reconnaissance at the battle of Maubeuge on 2nd June 1794. The French sent up the craft *Entreprenant* with two occupants to send down reports of the enemy's movements. The captain in charge was Jean Marie-Joseph Coutelle, appointed by Napoleon to form a balloon company, the first air corps in history. The first bombing raid was in 1849 when the Austrians sent a fleet of pilotless balloons to drop incendiary bombs on the beleaguered city of Venice. The bombs had time-fuses and did considerable damage. Balloons were used for military observation in the American Civil War, the Boer War and the First World War.

Attempts were made to propel balloons and to direct their flight. The envelope was elongated into a torpedo shape. In 1852, the French engineer Henri Giffard experimented with a small steam engine driving a propeller. There was not enough power to give more than some aid to steering. In 1884, a balloon was fitted with an electric motor and specially designed lightweight batteries. It reached a top speed of 22·5 kph (14 mph) on a round trip of five miles.

A great measure of control was achieved when the rigid airship was developed. In this, a streamlined hull contained a number of gas-bags, and nacelles to carry passengers and crew were slung underneath. Count von Zeppelin gave his name to a whole series of such aircraft. They were used in bombing raids in the First World War, but were too vulnerable to the swift fighter planes that had already been developed by then. Their use continued after the war, but the difficulty remained of providing sufficient lift. Hydrogen is the lightest gas, but it is highly inflammable and, mixed with air, explosive. This was the cause of a number of disasters. Helium, the inert gas discovered in 1895, was available only in small quantities and had but a quarter of the lifting power of hydrogen.

Ballooning, particularly the inexpensive hot-air variety, continues to be a popular sport today. Balloons, because of their silent movement, have been used to study the migrations of wild animals and for filming them from particular points of vantage. Sporting events are filmed from the air and small airships are being developed to carry awkward loads to sites that might otherwise be difficult to reach. We have not yet seen the end of the aerostatic machine, in which the balloonists of the 18th century were the first to travel.

October 1783—de Rozier and d'Arlandes take off in a Montgolfier hot-air balloon to become the first men to fly.

The Charles brothers in their hydrogen-filled balloon, 1783. Hydrogen-filled balloons have the advantage of being able to remain aloft almost indefinitely.

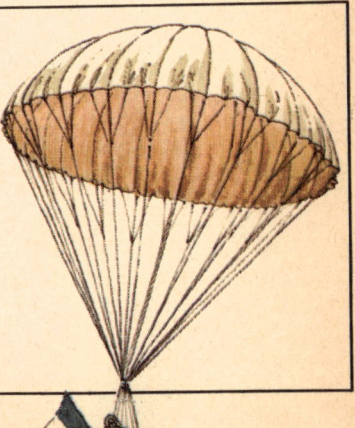

Garnerin makes the first parachute descent in 1797. The principle of the parachute was set down by Leonardo da Vinci, but it was not until the development of the aeroplane as a weapon that its use became widespread. In modern jet aircraft the pilot is ejected still in his seat, and his parachute opens automatically.

The Steam Engine

James Watt at work in his Glasgow laboratory

The idea of steam pressure as a motive force goes back to ancient times. Its practical realisation, however, came rather late in the progress of the Industrial Revolution. It had been known for some time that when heat converts water into steam its volume is expanded about 1,300 times. Thus, if steam is condensed back into water in a closed chamber, the result is a partial vacuum. Von Guericke demonstrated the force of atmospheric pressure on a vacuum. He produced a vacuum in a cylinder, one end of which was closed by a sliding piston. The strength of 50 men was unable to prevent the piston moving along the cylinder under the force of the atmospheric pressure outside it.

In France, in 1690, Denis Papin brought two principles together in a famous experiment. He put a little water in a cylinder with a moving piston. When the cylinder was heated to boil the water, steam pressure forced the piston to the top of the cylinder where a catch prevented it from being blown out. Jamming the piston in this position, Papin allowed the cylinder to cool. The steam condensed back into water, leaving a partial vacuum. When the piston was released, atmospheric pressure forced it rapidly down into the cylinder. Papin had created what should properly be called an atmospheric engine, since atmospheric pressure was the motive force.

The Miner's Friend

In 1698, the Englishman Thomas Savery patented an atmospheric engine which he described in a pamphlet entitled *The Miner's Friend*, since the engine's purpose was to pump water out of flooded mines. The essential part of Savery's engine was an oval-shaped vessel, at first filled with water. Steam entering this vessel forced out the water through an outlet valve which was closed as soon as the vessel was full of steam. Water from a tap was then poured over the vessel to condense the steam inside and produce a partial vacuum. A valve at the bottom was opened, and water from the flooded mine was forced in by the outside atmospheric pressure. The whole cycle then began again. There were two of these steam-condensing vessels working alternately. The operator, manually opening and shutting the valves at appropriate intervals, could work the engine at the rate of five cycles per minute.

Normal atmospheric pressure can

In 1698 Savery's 'miner's friend' used a combination of atmospheric pressure and superheated steam to reduce the water level in flooded coal mines.

The principle of the Newcomen engine. Steam at atmospheric pressure enters the cylinder from the bottom and is condensed by an injection of cold water. This creates a partial vacuum which draws the piston down.

raise a column of water only nine metres (30 feet) or so. Savery's engine had therefore to be built on a platform in the mineshaft about this distance above the flood water. To raise the water further, Savery used high-pressure steam. Water normally boils at about 100°C, the temperature at which the vapour pressure equals atmospheric pressure. In a closed vessel, the pressure above the water can be increased so that boiling takes place at a higher temperature. This is the principle of the pressure cooker, also invented by Denis Papin. Superheated water can generate very high pressures, for instance at 200°C steam pressure is fifteen times that of steam at 100°C. It would thus lift a column of water fifteen times higher than normal, about 135 metres (450 feet). Savery tried to use steam at eight to ten times atmospheric pressure, giving a potential lift of 90 metres (300 feet) or so. Unfortunately, construction problems associated with such high pressures could not, at that time, be overcome.

Newcomen's Engines

Meanwhile, Thomas Newcomen, a Devon man like Savery but working in Dartford, Kent, as a blacksmith and ironmonger, was independently developing his own invention. His engine used the cylinder and piston method suggested by Papin. The piston rod was attached to one end of a large beam pivoted in the middle like a pair of scales. The other end of the pump-rod brought the piston to the top of the cylinder. Steam at atmospheric pressure was introduced from the bottom of the cylinder until it was full. Then an injection-valve admitted a jet of cold water to condense the steam. Atmospheric pressure forced the piston down into the cylinder, now a partial vacuum, completing the cycle. Opening and shutting of steamcock and injection-valve were automatically controlled by movement of the injection-pump rod which was itself connected to the oscillating beam.

Newcomen's first operating engine was installed in the colliery at Dudley Castle in Worcestershire in 1712. The beam rocked twelve times a minute, lifting with every stroke 45 litres (ten gallons) of water 47 metres (153 feet) through a series of pumps. This invention spread rapidly through Britain, and by the time of the inventor's death in 1729 had reached many countries in Europe. Its drawback was the difficulty at the time of boring accurate cylinders. Newcomen tried to overcome this by sealing the top of the piston with a leather disc covered with a layer of water.

James Watt
James Watt was working as a maker of mathematical instruments at Glasgow University in Scotland when he was given a model of a Newcomen engine to repair. He saw that its efficiency was limited by the necessity of cooling the cylinder to condense the steam between strokes. He hit upon the idea of a separate condenser into which the steam could be drawn by means of an air-pump. In the engine he finally developed, the cylinder was kept hot by means of a steam-jacket. As the piston reached the top of its stroke, the exhaust valve at the bottom of the cylinder opened and, at the same time, steam was admitted to the space above the piston by an inlet valve. A combination of steam pressure and atmospheric pressure drove the piston down. At the bottom of its stroke, the exhaust and inlet valves were closed. A special valve opened to equalise the pressure on both sides of the piston which was drawn up again by the weight of the pump-rod. Watt went on to make his engines double-acting by admitting steam alternately on either side of the piston. He also cut off the supply of steam early in the stroke so that its expansion did the rest of the work. Watt can thus be credited with the invention of the steam engine as

The first locomotive to run on a track was built in 1804 by Richard Trevithick at Penydarran Ironworks in Wales. Trevithick was one of the first to use high-pressure steam.

George Stephenson (1781–1848) is regarded as the foremost engineer of the railway era.

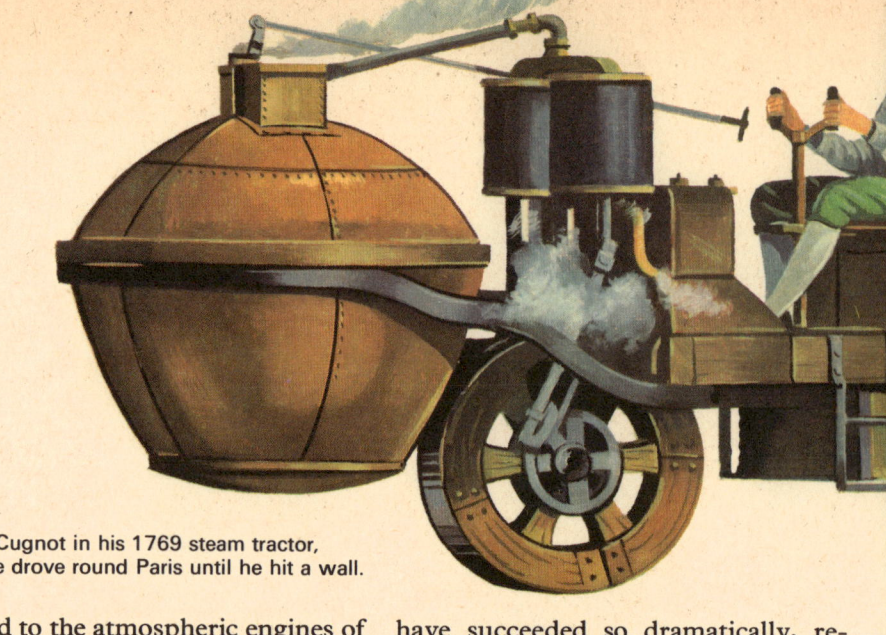

Nicolas Cugnot in his 1769 steam tractor, which he drove round Paris until he hit a wall.

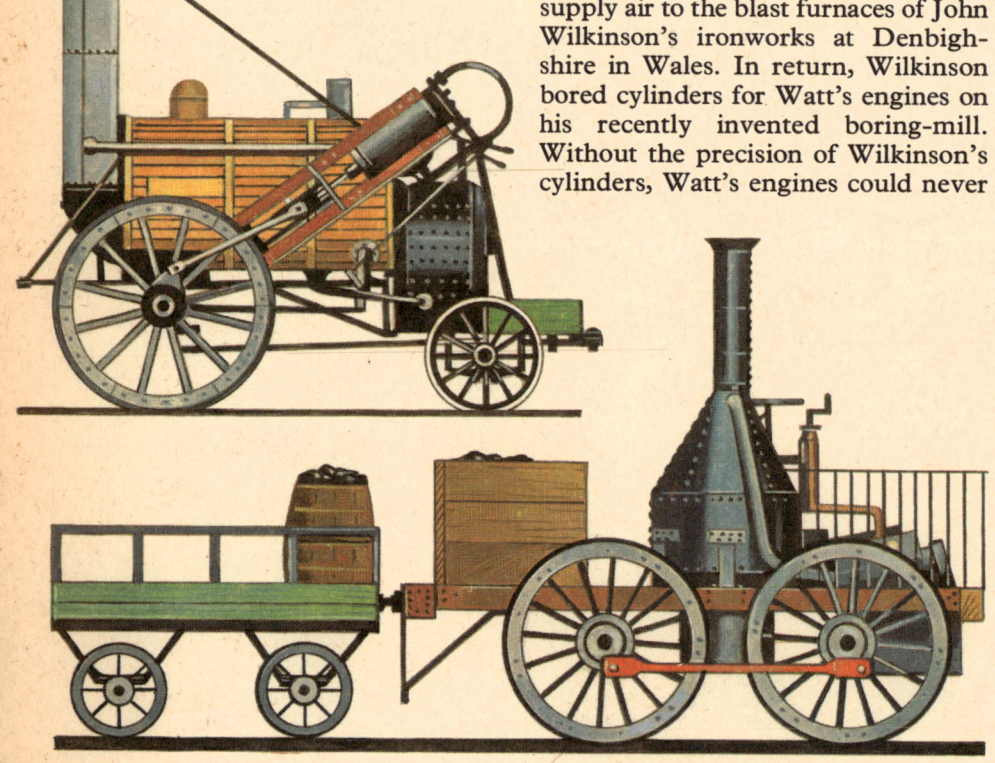

Top to bottom: the *Rocket*, George Stephenson's greatest engineering masterpiece, built in 1829; the *Best Friend of Charleston*, with a tender for carrying extra coal; and the *Novelty*, built by the Swede John Ericsson, with carriages.

opposed to the atmospheric engines of his predecessors.

It was May 1765 when Watt thought of the idea of a separate condenser, but 1776 before his first two engines began work. One of these was built to supply air to the blast furnaces of John Wilkinson's ironworks at Denbighshire in Wales. In return, Wilkinson bored cylinders for Watt's engines on his recently invented boring-mill. Without the precision of Wilkinson's cylinders, Watt's engines could never have succeeded so dramatically, requiring as they did airtight operation at high working temperatures. From the to and fro action of the engines used to power pumps, Watt naturally moved on to using rotary motion to power other machinery.

High-pressure Steam

Watt had always considered the use of high-pressure steam to be too dangerous. Almost at once, high-pressure steam engines were developed simultaneously in the United States and Britain. By 1804 in Philadelphia, Oliver Evans was using a small engine with a steam pressure of 50 pounds per square inch. Two years earlier, Richard Trevithick, a Cornish mine engineer, had built a pumping engine with a steam pressure of 145 pounds or ten times the normal pressure of the atmosphere. It was Trevithick who first produced a steam locomotive to run on a railway. In Wales in 1804, his locomotive pulled five trucks loaded with 70 men and ten tons of freight the sixteen kilometres (ten miles) or so between Penydarran ironworks and the Glamorganshire canal at a speed of eight kph (five mph). In 1808, he was charging the public five shillings a trip on a circular track near Euston Square in London.

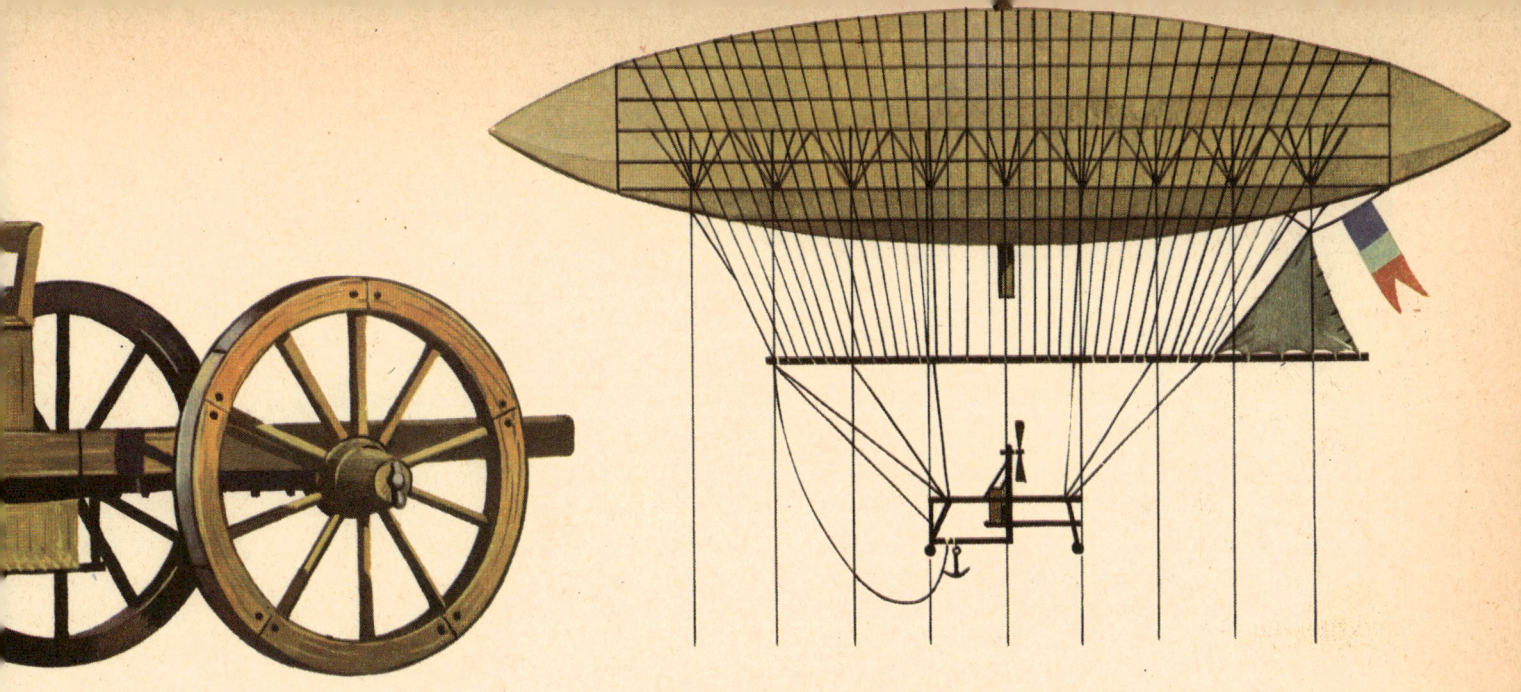

Giffard's airship, with a small steam engine driving a propeller, was too slow to steer.

The first powered vessel—the tug *Charlotte Dundas*, a paddle steamer built in Scotland in 1801–02.

The *Savannah*—first steamer across the Atlantic (1819). In fact she was a sailing ship with an auxiliary engine.

Above: the earliest Atlantic crossing under continuous steam power was by the packet-ship *Sirius*. It took 18½ days in 1838. Right: Robert Fulton's *Clermont* provided the first regular steamship service, on the River Hudson in 1807.

The development of the propeller was one of the most important advances in the history of the ship. Virtually all of the first steamships were powered by paddles arranged round wheels set either at the stern or on either side of the ship. At any given moment most of these paddlewheels is out of the water, and therefore doing no useful work. A propeller, on the other hand, is always totally immersed, so that almost all of the power fed into it through the driveshaft is used to push the ship forward. The picture shows the propeller of the *Great Britain*, one of Brunel's most famous designs, which is now being completely restored.

27

Industrial Progress

The joining of the Union Pacific and Central Pacific Railroads in 1869 gave the United States its first transcontinental rail link.

Transport

The railway was a very much earlier development than the steam locomotive. It was particularly used to ease the passage of coal trucks from pithead to canal. The motive power was either men or horses. The earliest rails were made of timber, which was first replaced by iron at Whitehaven in 1738. By 1767, cast-iron rails were being produced at Coalbrookdale, again in Britain, and their use began to spread. Both flanged rails for holding ordinary wheels on the track and flanged wheels on flat rails were early developments. Cast-iron is a rather brittle material, but from 1820 a method was devised for rolling wrought-iron rails which became the standard practice. In Britain, double-headed rails were keyed into special chairs fastened to the transverse wooden sleepers. In America, an inverted T-shape section was spiked directly into the sleepers.

The first public railway was a track for horse-drawn traffic which, by 1805, ran between Croydon and Wandsworth near London and was called the Surrey Iron Railway. In 1825, the opening of the Stockton to Darlington railway with steam locomotion began the world's modern railway system. By the 1840s in Britain, railway building had become a national mania. Steam engines improved in power and speed so rapidly that in 1849 there were five locomotives achieving average speeds of 80 kph (50 mph) between London and Bristol. Already, locomotives were happily coping with gradients of one in 38.

Signalling Systems

The increase in the railway network and the traffic that flowed along it required an elaborate signalling system. The French invention of the semaphore was adapted for the railways and used in conjunction with signal boxes placed at strategic intervals along the line. The first electric telegraph was installed between Paddington and West Drayton stations in 1839. Integrating the signal mechanism with that of the points first came into operation on the Hampstead Junction railway in 1859. Track was improved from 1862 when the first trials were made of steel rails at Crewe. All these developments took place in Britain but, by 1867, steel rails were being made in Pennsylvania for the rapidly expanding American network.

Early passenger coaches had four wheels or sometimes six. The bogie truck had been patented by an Englishman, William Chapman, in 1812. But the regular use of bogies at either end of a long passenger coach was an American invention. It made the coach able to take curves smoothly and avoided derailments on poorly aligned track. The Americans also led the way in passenger comfort with sleeping cars, dining cars and lavatory facilities.

The first American Pullman cars were imported into Britain in 1874, and one with electric lighting supplied by storage batteries was running between London and Brighton as early as 1881. Though Robert Stephenson invented a steam-brake in 1833, hand-brakes on tender or rear van were all that was deemed necessary for many years. During a test in 1875, the American Westinghouse compressed-air brake (first used in 1868) stopped a 200-ton train travelling at 80 kph (50 mph) in less than 300 metres (1,000 feet). Thereafter, the introduction of powered brakes not only avoided disasters but improved the timing of trains by making them pull up more quickly.

Roads and Waterways

The rapid expansion of the railway system in Britain replaced the horse-drawn coach-and-four sooner than in other countries. Yet road traffic increased in Britain as elsewhere, if only on short hauls from railway depots to town centres. The greatest world-wide influence on road-making was that of John Loudon McAdam (1756–1836), a Scot who had made his fortune in America and returned to his native Ayrshire. As Deputy Lieutenant of the county, he took an interest in the local roads. It was McAdam who established the principle that it was the native soil which bore the weight of traffic and, while it was kept dry, it would continue to bear the weight without sinking. He did away with the stone foundation, relying on the earth alone but making sure that there was good enough drainage to carry away any water or raising the road above water level. He also claimed that the thickness of the road was immaterial. What was needed was a waterproof and hard-wearing cover. He used small stones laid in three layers, each allowed to be compacted solidly by passing traffic. The macadamised surface spread throughout Europe and to America. Though nowadays his principles would be considered inadequate, his process was useful for repairing old surfaces.

In towns and cities, raised footpaths with stone kerbs began to appear in the second half of the 18th century. Roads carrying heavy traffic were covered with granite setts fitted together like masonry. Wood blocks were used in Russia at the beginning of the next century, and a creosoted type originated in America about 1867. Concrete road surfaces began in Austria in the 1850s and machinery for laying them was invented in Germany around 1879. The development of the asphalt road was carried on in France from 1832 with a mixture of powdered rock asphalt and bitumen from natural oil seepages. Sand-asphalt applied at temperatures between 150° and 200°C, and spread and rolled while still hot, provided a watertight surface. Tarmac, a mixture of coal-tar and small stones also laid hot and consolidated after cooling with a thin coat of sand, was first used in Britain in the 1830s. Such hot rolled surfaces became important, however, only when fast motor vehicles with rubber tyres began to break up macadamised surfaces.

Despite the growth of road and rail networks in the 19th century, canals and rivers did not lose their importance as means of transport. A great deal of work was done on European rivers bypassing rapids, deepening shallows and even straightening the watercourse. Some of this was laborious pick and shovel cutting and embanking. Sometimes a rough course was cut and the river turned into it to do the rest of the work, often with unintended results. Work on the great St Lawrence Seaway in Canada began in 1821 when the 13·5 metre (46-foot) Lachine falls were bypassed. The Welland canal was dug to bypass Niagara Falls and by 1847 the route from Montreal to Lake Ontario was completed. Between 1817 and 1824, the 585-kilometre (364-mile) Erie canal was built, linking New York with the Great Lakes. The 164-kilometre (102-mile) Morris canal in New York state had 23 inclined planes up which barges were hauled, mounted on a trolley which in its turn was pulled up rails by a cable-drum operated from a water wheel. For the digging of Ferdinand de Lesseps's Suez Canal, opened in 1869, a trough-dredger with long

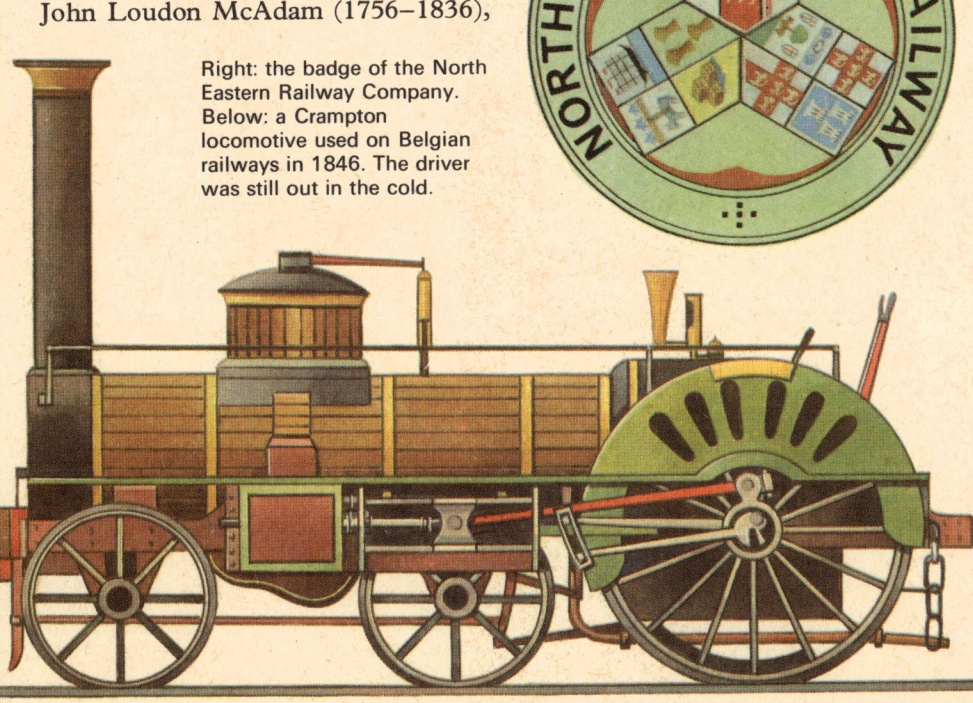

Right: the badge of the North Eastern Railway Company. Below: a Crampton locomotive used on Belgian railways in 1846. The driver was still out in the cold.

A railway navvy, 'ready for anything'. Navvies often lived for years in camps which moved with the railhead all over the country.

Techniques of road-building have kept pace with increasing numbers and weights of vehicles. Three early surfaces were (left to right) those of Telford, McAdam, Tresaguet.

Suspension bridges have to be specially reinforced to resist the pressure of side winds. The Brooklyn Bridge was one of the first to use the Roebling technique.

chutes for depositing silt was devised. A floating sand-pump was invented, and chisel-pointed rams broke up the rock. By 1867, 60 dredgers were moving 1·5 million cubic metres (56 million cubic feet) a month.

Bridge-building

In the techniques of bridge-building, there were a number of important improvements, stimulated by the growth of rail and road networks. In 1830, Sir Thomas Cochrane (later tenth Earl of Dundonald) introduced compressed-air caissons for the building of foundations on marshy ground. The principle was to lower a chamber on to the river bed and pump air into it to counter-balance the pressure of water outside. The men digging inside passed the waste up through an airlock. As the caisson sank so it was built upwards to maintain a height always above water level.

Suspension bridges were built with longer and longer spans. There were many collapses until it was realised that the suspended deck needed reinforcement to avoid excessive movement in high winds. The most important advance was made by John Roebling, a German immigrant to America, with an arrangement of wire cable patented in 1841. Previous wire ropes were weakened by the twisting together of individual wires. Roebling proposed instead bundles of thick wires bound together after hanging. For the Brooklyn Bridge in New York, loops of galvanised steel wire were hauled across in both directions. Men on catwalks adjusted them for correct level and uniform sag. Then they were bunched into four main cables and bound together.

The cantilever system, in which the main structure is built outward from both sides and the intervening space linked by a girder span, was known in a crude form to the Chinese from ancient times. The system was fully employed in the Firth of Forth railway bridge in Scotland in which three main piers were established and each extended on either side simultaneously to preserve the balance. The 107-metre (350-foot) gaps between the cantilevered arms of the main piers were then built out to meet in the middle. When the ends came to be joined, such precision was achieved that improvised packing only was needed to expand the metal slightly to enable the final bolts to be inserted.

Tunnelling

An improved method of tunnelling through soft materials such as sand was introduced with Marc Brunel's shield used in the first tunnel constructed under the Thames in London and opened in 1843. It had two intermediate platforms enabling 36 men on three levels to attack the face simultaneously. It was moved forward a short distance at a time by jacks working against the completed masonry behind it. For the Mont Cenis tunnel through the Alps, a distance of twelve kilometres (eight miles) through solid rock, gunpowder was used for blasting and pneumatic drills were operated by water-powered compressors. The rate of advance, working from both ends, was 0·8 of a kilometre (half a mile) a year. The St Gothard tunnel, completed twelve years later in 1882, doubled this rate by using rock-drilling machinery from the start and the new dynamite for blasting.

Using a boring machine in the Mont Cenis tunnel, 1856–71.

Engineering

Power looms in a factory. The development of machinery to perform the repetitive tasks of weaving brought about enormous reductions in manufacturing costs.

Eli Whitney (1765–1825), American inventor of the cotton gin. He made very little money from his invention, and later manufactured the first muskets to have standardised interchangeable parts.

Perhaps the most important technological development in machine engineering in the 19th century was what has come to be known as the American system of interchangeable parts. It had begun, in fact, in Europe as a means of increasing production of muskets. The parts of the flintlock mechanism were designed for mass-production with sufficient precision to make assembly a comparatively unskilled job. In the United States, Eli Whitney, who had been unable to make sufficient profits from his cotton gin patented in 1794, turned to the production of muskets on the same principle. At a factory near New Haven in Connecticut, Whitney began making muskets using the new methods in 1798. Progress was slow at the beginning as machines had first to be invented and then built which would turn out uniform parts. When the government grew impatient, Whitney pointed out that once the machines were made and operating the assembly of the guns would be a simple and speedy matter. To prove his point he assembled a number of muskets before government representatives with parts chosen by them at random from piles of spares.

The idea of interchangeable parts spread to all small arms. Samuel Colt, inventor of the revolver, by 1853 had a factory using 1,400 machine-tools. As the century advanced, the system was used in all newly invented machines for which there was a mass demand. America, chronically short of skilled labour, continued to lead the way, pouring out cheaply manufactured machinery of increasing sophistication such as harvesters, sewing-machines and typewriters.

Textile Factories

In factories, mechanisation continued to develop, particularly in the textile industry where much of it had begun. Steam power was at first used to pump water for the operation of wheels which drove the actual machinery. In time, more and more steam engines were used to drive the machines directly. All the processes of preparation of raw materials, spinning, weaving and finishing off the cloth gradually surrendered to the mighty machine. Even the allied trades of hosiery, knitting and lacemaking began to be mechanised.

In Britain, John Heathcoat, a frame-smith in the hosiery industry, invented the first satisfactory lace-making machine in 1809. John Leavers adapted the Heathcoat machine to make patterned lace in 1813. Finally, about 1840, Hooton Deverill in Nottingham made the first successful application of the Jacquard loom to lace-making. Net curtains appeared at every window and lace peeped from every petticoat.

Mechanisation of the knitting process for the making of stockings was longer delayed. In the 1840s Matthew Townsend of Leicester invented a circular rib-frame for making non-fashioned seamless hose. But it was William Cotton of Loughborough who produced a machine capable of making a dozen hose simultaneously and knitting fashioned garments of various kinds. At last, in 1887, inventors in America produced a power-driven sewing machine which could provide

When the manufacture of textiles ceased to be a craft industry and became a matter of tending machines, the employment of child labour became widespread. It was common for a child to work for twelve hours per day.

a seam for any knitted garment, working at 3,000 stitches a minute. Before this Elias Howe, a Massachusetts mechanic, had invented the lock-stitch, the principle on which sewing machines were developed. His machine could sew only straight seams of limited length. In 1851, Isaac M. Singer of Boston produced the first practical domestic sewing machine using a straight needle and worked by a foot-treadle. The same year, the alternative chain-stitch was invented.

A draw-loom had been used in Kidderminster as early as 1735 for the weaving of carpet. Ninety years later, the Jacquard loom was adapted for the same purpose. The big breakthrough came when E. B. Bigelow of Massachusetts invented his Brussels power-loom. Strong wires with looped ends were automatically inserted and withdrawn to raise the looped pile, while thinner wires with a knife blade at the end raised and then cut the loops to produce the thick pile. The machine was improved in England to produce the famous Wilton carpet.

Machine-tool Industry

An important innovation in the machine-tool industry was the American invention of the turret lathe in the 1840s. A number of different tools could be locked into the octagonal turret which the operator could rotate to bring each tool in turn to bear upon the workpiece. Within twenty years, a mechanism was in use to rotate the turret automatically so that the lathe could go through a series of operations without further attention. At the same time, a means was devised of feeding in further metal bars to be worked without stopping the lathe. The way was open to a fully automatic lathe, machining a number of components simultaneously.

Precision Tools

These same principles were applied to drilling machinery. In 1862, Nasmyth produced a slot-drilling machine which was a valuable innovation. Previously, slots could be cut in metal only by boring two round holes and chipping away the metal in between. Further developments were in large vertical boring machines in which the part to be worked was clamped in a horizontal rotating table. About 1862, the first fully effective milling machine was designed in America by Joseph Brown. It was originally made to cut the spiral grooves in a twist-drill, but was quickly adapted to many other uses previously requiring hand-work. It eventually led, in the 1870s, to the automatic cutting of gearwheels which were beginning to play such an important part in the development of all machines, particularly as faster operation was the continual aim. Great advances in industrial development were made possible by the precision of the new machine tools. Watt's partner, Matthew Boulton, was so impressed with the accuracy of a cylinder bored by John Wilkinson in 1776 that he remarked it 'doth not err the thickness of an old shilling'. Yet Joseph Whitworth's machine, invented in 1856, was capable of measuring to one-millionth of an inch (·0000025 centimetres)—an extraordinary advance in precision.

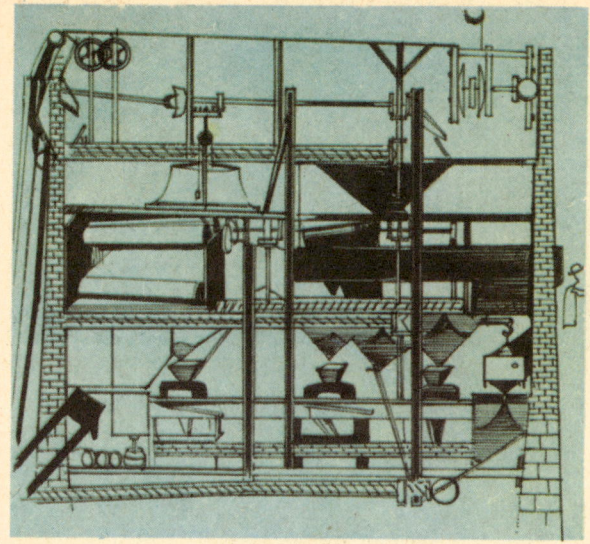

Oliver Evans (1755–1819), the American inventor of grain handling machinery, and a diagram of his flour mill. Evans also designed steam engines.

Luddites, 1811. Fear that the new textile machinery was jeopardising jobs led to violent riots and the destruction of several mills. This riot is led by a man dressed as a woman.

The Chemical Industry

New dyes for new fashions. The 'mauve decade' of the 1890s.

William Perkin's first synthetic dye.

The Industrial Revolution created a demand for large supplies of chemicals, particularly for the cleaning and bleaching of textiles, for glass-making and for soap-boiling. The demand was to create the modern chemical industry. One material in short supply, particularly in France, was soda. The French Academy offered a prize in 1775 for a method of making soda from salt. The problem was solved in 1787 by Nicolas Leblanc, physician to the Duke of Orleans. In his process, common salt was treated with sulphuric acid and the resulting sodium sulphate mixed with coal and limestone. The mixture was roasted and the soda extracted from the 'black ash' with water. The solution was evaporated in the atmosphere in open pans.

A purer product, for use in glass-making for instance, could be obtained by crystallisation.

Though he opened factories at St Denis, Rouen and Lille, Leblanc was dispossessed by the revolution and committed suicide in poverty in 1806. James Muspratt brought the process to Britain, though the soap-boilers who eventually became his best customers were suspicious of synthetic soda. Muspratt had to give it away at first and even supervise its use. In 1828, Muspratt formed a partnership with Josias Gamble and they set up a new works in St Helens, Lancashire, which has ever since been a centre of the British chemical industry. In 1825, Charles Tennant began manufacturing soda by the Leblanc method in Glasgow where his St Rollox works became the biggest chemical factory in Europe. By the 1830s it employed 1,000 workers, covered 40 hectares (100 acres) of land and had a chimney 139 metres (455 feet) high which was a famous local landmark.

Acid Production

Sulphuric acid played an important part in the production of synthetic soda. The centre for its manufacture has long been Nordhausen in Saxony where it was distilled from green vitriol (ferrous sulphate). But the process was expensive. In 1737, Joshua Ward began manufacture in Britain at Richmond by burning sulphur and saltpetre in the necks of glass vessels containing a little water. As the water became dilute sulphuric acid, it was concentrated by distillation. He reduced the price of the acid from £2 to two shillings a pound (0·4 kilogram). John Roebuck improved on the process by replacing the glass vessels with chambers made of lead, one of the few cheap metals resistant to sulphuric acid. Lead chamber factories were built in Rouen, France, in 1766 and in Philadelphia in the United States in 1793.

The original process was quickly improved. The quantity of saltpetre required was reduced by increasing the supply of air to the combustion process which was transferred to separate furnaces. Steam jets replaced the shallow layers of water in the lead chambers. By 1830, the price of sulphuric acid had been brought down to $2\frac{1}{2}$ pence a pound.

The Leblanc soda-making process produced clouds of hydrochloric acid gas which is an unpleasant and destructive pollutant. In 1836, William Gossage, a Worcestershire chemical manufacturer, invented a tower in which the gas was absorbed in falling water. The resulting hydrochloric acid became a valuable by-product since its use had already been established in the manufacture of bleaching powder. The traditional way of bleaching textiles had been treatment with buttermilk and exposure to sunlight, a slow process taking months to complete. In

Early matches. Phosphorus content produced 'phossy jaw', a lethal disease caused by handling it.

1785, the French chemist Berthollet showed that passing chlorine through potash made a solution with a strong bleaching action. In 1799, Tennant improved the process by passing chlorine over lime. The production of cheap bleaching powder gave a boost to the cotton industry without which it could not have expanded so rapidly.

Synthetic Dyes

A later, important development in the chemical and textile industries was the replacement of vegetable with synthetic dyes. This began when the German chemist August Wilhelm von Hofmann went to London in 1845 to be the first superintendent of the Royal College of Chemistry. Hofmann was interested in the chemical composition of coal-tar, a substance becoming cheaply available from the growing gas industry. He found a way of obtaining aniline cheaply from nitrobenzene, a coal-tar product, though he had no idea what could be made of it. A student of his, William Perkin, experimenting with aniline in the hope of producing quinine, found himself with some purple crystals which could be used to dye silk a brilliant mauve. By 1857, Perkin had his own works near Harrow to produce the first synthetic dyes.

Explosives

Alongside the dyestuffs industry, developments were taking place in explosives. Up to the middle of the 19th century the only important explosive for both military and civil engineering use was gunpowder. C. F. Schönbein discovered that cellulose treated with nitric acid produced an

Alfred Nobel (1833–96), famous both for the invention of dynamite and the prizes named after him. The Peace Prize medal is shown.

explosive material. It was called guncotton because cotton was the source of the cellulose. In 1846, it was manufactured in Britain by Schönbein in association with John Hall and Sons of Faversham but a disastrous explosion put an end to the enterprise. Nitroglycerine, discovered by the Italian chemist, A. Sobrero, was also a dangerous explosive to handle. It was Alfred Nobel who made it safe by absorbing it in a clay called Kieselguhr. His product became known as dynamite. Handled with reasonable care it is perfectly safe, but can be exploded by the use of a detonator such as fulminate of mercury.

Another chemical industry was the manufacture of artificial fertiliser. Treating bones or mineral phosphate with sulphuric acid produces superphosphate, one of the most important agricultural fertilisers. It was manufactured by James Murray in Dublin from 1817. The large-scale industrial production of superphosphate was begun in 1834 by John Bennet Lawes in a factory at Deptford Creek near London. With J. H. Gilbert, he carried out extensive experiments on his agricultural estate at Rothamsted.

The chemical industry was also to bring important contributions to the field of medicine. Nitrous oxide, made by heating ammonium nitrate, was first used to alleviate pain in 1844 by a Connecticut dentist, Horace Wells. An American surgeon, C. W. Long, was the first to use ether in a minor operation. Its volatile nature, however, led Long to search for a substitute which resulted in the discovery of chloroform. In Britain, the pioneer work of Joseph Lister in the use as antiseptic of carbolic acid obtained from the distillation of coal-tar eventually led to the general use of iodine from 1878.

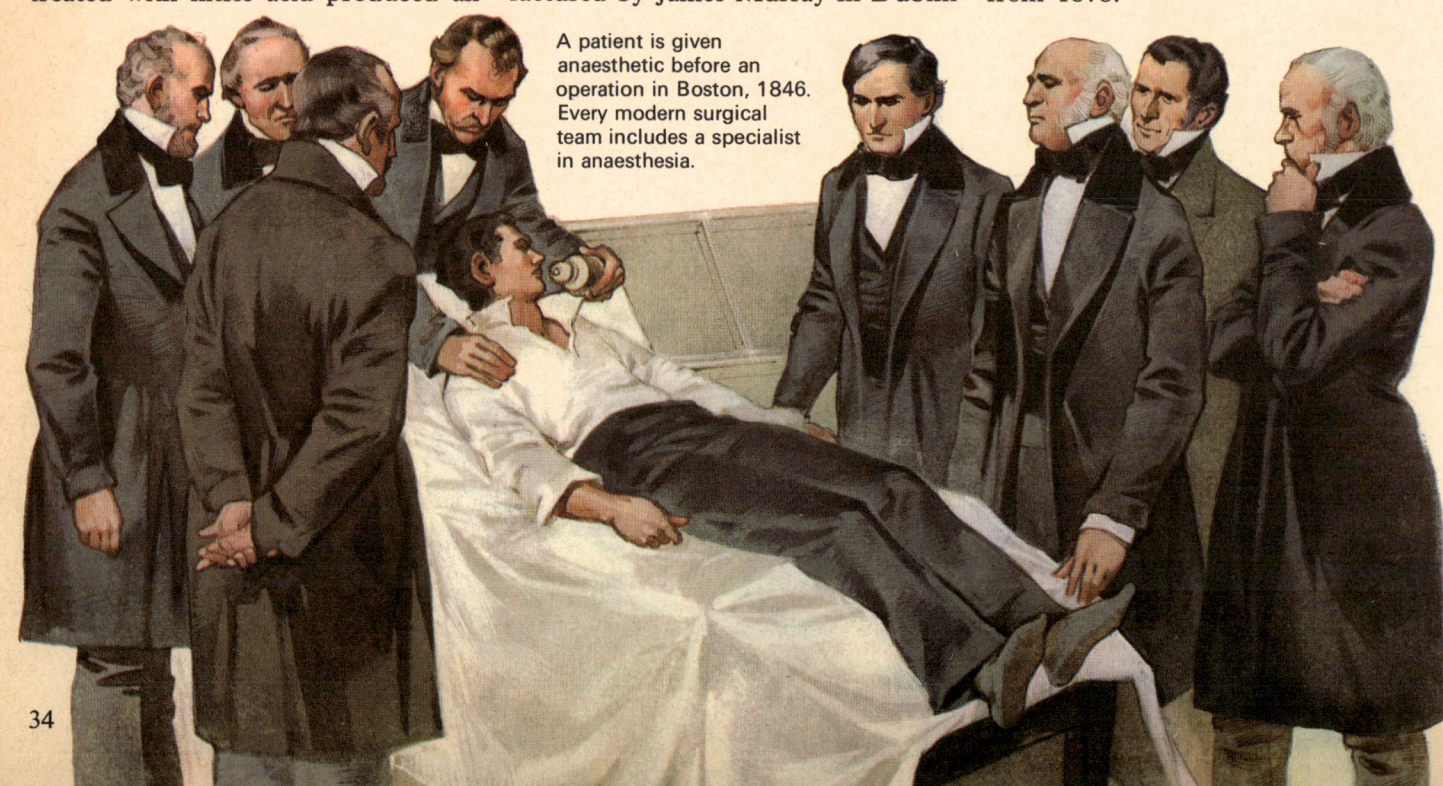

A patient is given anaesthetic before an operation in Boston, 1846. Every modern surgical team includes a specialist in anaesthesia.

Rubber

A material that was slow to be absorbed within the general progress of the Industrial Revolution was rubber. It had been known to Europeans since the discoverers of the New World had found natives cutting rubber tree bark and collecting the latex that oozed from the wound. The difficulty was doing anything with such an elastic material after it had coagulated and dried into a solid shape. Caoutchouc, as the substance was called, was brought back in the form of bottle-shapes or large balls, but could not easily be reformed into anything else. In 1770, Joseph Priestley found use for it in rubbing out pencil marks. In France, at the time of the revolution, it was softened with oil and wrapped round a bar to produce tubes useful to surgeons. In Britain, there was some experimentation in waterproof fabrics and air-beds. Rubberised fabric was used for a balloon in 1783.

Sheet Rubber

It was Thomas Hancock who first began to achieve some success with invention of his masticator in 1820. This consisted of a hollow cylinder with a solid roller inside which produced cylinders of rubber that could be pressed in iron moulds to any desired shape or size. Hancock began to make sheet rubber by shaving slices off a block. Slices could be joined by warming them and laying them edge to edge. Rubber thread was made by cutting rubber tubes spirally on a lathe. These could be used to make elastic webbing. Hancock also experimented with mixtures of rubber and tar which gave a cheaper product.

The Macintosh

Charles Macintosh, a Glasgow chemical manufacturer, first found a suitable solvent for rubber in coal-tar naphtha. Rubber dissolved in naphtha made a waterproof varnish that could be brushed on to cloth. By making a sandwich of two layers of cloth with the rubber coating between them, a tacky surface was avoided. Macintoshes were first produced in a Manchester factory opened in 1824. Hancock improved Macintosh's process by using masticated rubber. In partnership with Macintosh, he invented a machine for making rubberised fabrics.

Charles Goodyear, a Philadelphia hardware merchant, experimented with rubber and found that heating it with sulphur produced a substance no longer affected by heat or cold. The process was called vulcanisation. It allowed a lighter waterproof garment to be made. Vulcanised rubber was ideal for shoes, conveyor-belting and hoses. By the middle of the century, Hancock was manufacturing rubber tyres for road vehicles. These were solid and attached by metal hoops or stretched and held in position by a flange. A patent was taken out in the 1840s for pneumatic rubber tyres with an outer casing of leather. Known as aerial wheels, they were tested successfully in Hyde Park, London, and in New York. Yet the invention was completely forgotten until J. B. Dunlop's bicycle tyres of 1888. Michelin produced his first motor tyre in 1895 and Dunlop his in 1900. Fortunes were made in durable rubber compounds until synthetics replaced them.

J. B. Dunlop (1840–1921), who took out a patent for his pneumatic bicycle tyre in 1888. He made a fortune from the enormous popularity of cycling and, later, motoring.

Charles Macintosh (1766–1843), inventor of the rubberised waterproof cloth which still bears his name.

An 1895 Lutzmann with solid rubber tyres. The body is sprung independently of the chassis.

Coal-gas and Oil

Coal-gas, as fire-damp, had long been a hazard to miners. It was the year 1760 before an attempt was made to light a room with it in a house in Newcastle. The gas was produced in a kettle and passed along the stem of a clay tobacco pipe. It was ignited at holes made in the clay. A French engineer, Philippe Lebon, took out a patent in 1799 for lighting from the gas obtained by heating wood. James Watt's son, Gregory, went to Paris even though his country was at war with France, to investigate. Already in 1792 an engineer working for the firm Boulton and Watt, William Murdock, had used coal gas to light the rooms of a house in Redruth, Cornwall. Called back to the firm's Soho works in Birmingham, Murdock lit the main building there for several nights. By 1804, the firm was ready to look for customers for Murdock's process. In 1806–7, a large Salford cotton mill had 900 gas lights installed in the factory, along a stretch of private road and in a private house.

Large-scale Lighting

Having got into the business on the ground floor, so to speak, it is surprising that in 1814 Boulton and Watt decided to give up. From that year, Murdock is no longer associated with the story. Instead, it passes to Samuel Clegg who had been apprenticed to Boulton and Watt but had left the firm in 1805. It was Clegg who made the first important improvement by putting lime in the water through which the gas passed in the retort thus ridding it of its unpleasant smell. He was also installing gas lighting in factories. He fitted it in the premises of Rudolph Ackermann, the London art publisher, who had two cast-iron retorts with a capacity of a hundredweight of coal each, serving 80 burners for both lighting and heating.

A lecture on gas lighting in a London theatre, showing the retort used to provide gas for the burners. Although the first attempt to use gas for illumination was made in 1760, it was not until 1814 that the idea was pursued on a large scale.

In 1808 Pall Mall in London became the first street to be lit by gas.

The idea of a central generating station to distribute gas throughout a whole district was first devised in 1806 by a German immigrant to Britain, F. A. Winsor (formerly Winzer). In 1812 he was given a charter for his Gas Light and Coke Company and shortly afterwards secured the services of Samuel Clegg. On 1st April 1814, the parish of St Margaret's in Westminster was lit by gas. By the end of 1816, London had 42 kilometres (26 miles) of gas-mains. In the same year Baltimore began gas lighting in the streets and was followed by Boston and New York. Gas lighting began in Paris with the Palais Royal in 1819. A British company introduced it into Berlin in 1826, and by 1866 it had reached Moscow.

Heating and Cooking

As early as 1802, a Moravian, Z. A. Winzler, inspired by Lebon, was giving dinner parties with food cooked on a gas-stove in a dining room heated by gas. But gas cooking and the heating of water with geysers was a rarity until the 1870s. By then, the gas companies were approaching the time when there was serious competition from electricity. As an illuminant, coal-gas's smoky flame was saved from extinction by the incandescent gas-mantle invented in the 1880s by an Austrian, C. A. von Welsbach.

This was a gauze cap impregnated with thorium oxide and a little cerium oxide which gave a cleaner, brighter light. It carried gas lighting into the 20th century when the companies began to concentrate on selling their produce for heating and cooking, where it still functions efficiently.

Petroleum Products

Petroleum products from the earth's natural seepages have a very ancient history. Our concern here is with their application to the period of the Industrial Revolution. The demand was for improved lighting which had stimulated the gas industry. Oil lamps became more efficient after 1783 with the introduction of a flat-woven wick. Later there came the circular oil-burner with a cylindrical wick and glass chimney, named the Argand after its inventor. But the introduction of gas lighting served only to emphasise the poor quality of both the vegetable and animal oils available.

In 1848, James Young began to develop a lubricant from a spring of crude oil that appeared for a short time in a Derbyshire coal mine. Later, he manufactured paraffin oil by dry distillation from a brown shale called torbanite, but again supplies of the raw material ran out. In the late 1850s, he was selling 'paraffin illuminating oil' made from coal tar naphtha, while American competitors were making so-called 'coal-oil' from an asphalt-like mineral found in New Brunswick, Canada.

Meanwhile, Abraham Gesner, a London doctor interested in geology, took out patents for a distillation of asphalt rock which produced a liquid that could be purified by treatment with sulphuric acid and lime and then redistilled. This new oil, called kerosene, sold well together with a new lamp with a flat wick and a chimney. Gesner hoped that it would completely replace whale-oil. The situation was entirely changed, however, in 1859 by the drilling of the first American oil well.

Oil Drilling

In the early part of the century, drilling had been undertaken in the search for salt or for water. In 1830, the introduction of the derrick made drilling easier and, by 1850, the steam

The first oil rig in Pennsylvania, 1859. Although previous rigs had frequently struck oil when drilling to find salt, it had never been extracted because at that time it had no commercial value.

engine was being used as a source of power. Between 1840 and 1860 in America, borings in search of salt had, on at least fifteen occasions, struck petroleum. The American industrialist, G. H. Bissell, began to consider the possibility of deliberately boring for oil. In 1854, he sent a sample of oil from a natural Pennsylvanian seepage to Benjamin Silliman Jr, professor of chemistry at Yale university. Silliman's report showed that by heating the crude oil in a still, several new products apart from illuminating gas, paraffin wax, lubricants and lamp-oil could be obtained. Bissell therefore ordered his contractor, Edwin L. Drake, to go ahead. After drilling through only 21 metres (69 feet) of bedrock, oil was struck on 27th August 1859 and the great Pennsylvania oil field had begun. Within fifteen years, annual output had reached ten million 163-kg (360-pound) barrels. In the years that followed, hollow drilling pipes could remove samples to reveal the structure of underground rock formations so that prospecting for oil became independent of chance oil seepages on the surface. Methods of refining to maintain the maximum yield of products from particular varieties of crude oil also advanced rapidly.

Victorian improvements such as the cylindrical wick and the chimney greatly increased the efficiency of oil lamps.

Steel

The discovery of another great raw material for industry was also made in America though its inventor gained nothing from it and is hardly remembered today. Iron had served its turn in the Industrial Revolution. The need now arose for a cheap steel of uniform quality for the new generation of precision machines and instruments. William Kelly was a manufacturer of sugar-kettles for farmers in Kentucky. His pig-iron was refined in a charcoal furnace, but the price of charcoal was rising even in timber-rich America. Kelly made the accidental discovery that a blast of air playing on molten pig-iron produced more heat when the iron was not covered with charcoal. The carbon in the pig-iron could therefore be blown out by air alone, the carbon already present acting as the fuel. By retaining more of the carbon than was needed for wrought iron, this air-boiling process could be used to make a steel.

The quantity of carbon retained in the iron is what gives steel its hardness. This had been realised by the Swedish metallurgist, T. O. Bergmann, as early as 1750. It is therefore surprising that Kelly's process had not been discovered before. But making steel from pig-iron without fuel seemed absurd to the ironmasters of the day. From 1851 onwards, Kelly built a series of converters and patented his invention in 1857. In the same year, he went bankrupt, and his patents fell into the hands of Henry Bessemer in Britain.

The Bessemer Process

Bessemer was a prolific inventor who had made a fortune from his patent of a process for making gold leaf cheaply. Another of his discoveries was a method of casting sheets of glass. The demand for new ways of casting cannon during the Crimean War (1854–6) had interested Bessemer in the subject of steel manufacture. Steel had been produced in small quantities for some time but the process made it very expensive.

Bessemer had been working on the same lines of 'boiling' the molten iron with a strong blast of air. In 1860, he invented his famous tilting converter. During the actual conversion of the molten iron into steel, the blast of air comes from the bottom and is forced right through the molten metal. When the metal is being run in or out of the converter, the 'wind box' is swung up to the top where it is out of action.

Open-hearth Furnaces

In 1861, Frederick Siemens invented a gas-producer which used low-grade coal to produce a gas that could be used as a fuel. His patent stated the possibility of using the invention to melt steel in an open-hearth furnace. It led to making steel from mixtures of cast iron and malleable iron called the Siemens-Martin process, and the decarburising of cast iron with iron ore to make steel which is called the Siemens process. These open-hearth systems had the advantage of attaining very high working temperatures. They were economic because scrap iron and cheap coal were used. They were comparatively slow processes so they were more easily and strictly controlled.

The majority of the iron in Britain is phosphoric, and non-phosphoric iron had to be imported from Scandinavia in order for the new process to work satisfactorily.

Both the Bessemer and the Siemens processes needed to use ores containing no phosphorous. Getting rid of phosphorous was a discovery made by S. G. Thomas and his cousin, Percy Gilchrist. They included limestone with the firebricks and this combined with the phosphorous to form a slag. The slag could be easily removed and, incidentally, could be pulverised to

Bessemer's design for a hydraulically stabilised ship's saloon. The idea was never put to the test.

Henry Bessemer (1813–98), and a Bessemer converter in action.

The Bessemer conversion process. Molten pig iron is run into the converter, and air is blown through it. This oxidises the impurities in the iron, releasing heat which keeps the mass molten.

When conversion is complete, the converter is tilted and the molten steel pours out.

form the basis of a valuable agricultural fertiliser. The cousins' process virtually doubled the world's steel production.

Rolling Mills

With the increase in the supply of cheap steel, the development of rolling mills was not far behind. From these came the bars, sections and plates for the construction industry. The universal mill which began to appear from 1884 had enormous power. It could take an unhammered cast-steel ingot and convert it into a plate or a bar of any required width. Plates were produced for boilers and the new iron and steel ships, even heavy armour plate for the warship. By the turn of the century, the great Krupp's steelworks in Germany could take a thick steel ingot weighing more than 130 tonnes and roll it into a thinner plate measuring about three by thirteen metres (eleven by forty-three feet).

For a time, the South Wales and Monmouthshire steelworks had the virtual monopoly of the production of tinplate. For this, steel was rolled to a thickness of ·025 centimetres (one-hundredth of an inch). Hot rolled sheets were annealed, pickled and immersed in oil before dipping in the molten tin. They were then rolled again to regulate the thickness of the tin covering which even in best quality tinplate was less than ·0005 centimetres (one five-thousandth of an inch). As tinplate rusted quickly out of doors and was used mainly for food containers and the like, another sheet metal was developed. This was galvanised iron in which the sheet was dipped in molten zinc. Galvanised wire was used for fencing, often as barbed-wire.

Steel Alloys

Steels alloyed with other metals were at first produced accidentally by the smelting of mixed ores. Faraday made experimental samples of chromium and nickel steel as early as 1819. Tungsten steel was produced by the Austrian, F. Köller, in 1858. Ten years later R. F. Mushet, an ironmaster from the Forest of Dean, was manufacturing high-carbon tungsten-manganese steel which gave tools made from it five or six times the life of ordinary steel. Chromium steel for armour plate and shells was produced in France from 1877. Manganese steel, hardened from a temperature of 1000°C by quenching in water, was discovered by Robert Hadfield in Sheffield. Nickel steel was produced by the Le Creusot ironworks in France from 1888. F. W. Taylor of Philadelphia invented a high-speed steel that became harder the faster it cut.

Between 1870 and the end of the century, the world output of steel had grown from half a million to 28 million tons. Most of the growth was in America, where began the period producing a quarter of Britain's output and ended it producing double the British total. Together with the addition of electrical power to the earlier steam power, steel was the dynamic of the latter half of the Industrial Revolution, its various forms contained in all the busy tools and humming machines of the world's manufactories.

The Specialist Scientists

Dalton lecturing on his atomic theory.

The Structure of the Atom

While the engineers and inventors were busy advancing their various technologies, scientists were beginning to specialise in different aspects of the physical world. In the 16th century Vesalius had begun to list the elements of which all matter is composed. The next step was to discover the parts of an element and what made one element behave differently from another. The ancient Greeks had put forward the idea of atoms, tiny indestructible particles so small that in solids and liquids there seemed to be no space between them. Aristotle and Plato were against the idea. It fell into disrepute throughout the later years of antiquity and the Middle Ages. It was not revived again until the 17th century when men like Descartes and Newton began to explain phenomena in terms of the mutual interaction and movement of particles.

Dalton's Atomic Theory

The man who devised the primitive structure on which modern atomic theory rests was John Dalton (1766–1844). He was the largely self-educated son of a Cumberland hand-weaver and became a teacher of mathematics in the New College of Manchester. He was a member of the Literary and Philosophical Society of Manchester and later became its secretary and president. It was his ideas rather than his personality that brought him fame. As a lecturer he was not good at devising the kind of experimental demonstration which impressed the audiences of so many contemporary scientists. When he did include a demonstration, his experiments often went wrong.

In 1803, he began to apply his conception of atoms to chemical analysis. He decided that the difference between the atoms of different elements might be a difference of size and weight. He showed that eight parts by weight of oxygen combined with one part of hydrogen to form water. Assuming that a compound atom (now called a molecule) of water consisted of one atom of hydrogen and one of oxygen, it followed that the atomic weight of oxygen was eight times that of hydrogen. We now know that *two* atoms of hydrogen combine with one of oxygen to form water. Dalton's estimate of the atomic weight of oxygen was thus half the true value. Yet his theory led him to draw up the first table of atomic weights. He was correct in thinking that all atoms of the same element have the same weight, and that the compound atoms of any particular substance always contain the same number and kinds of atoms.

Chemical Symbols

Dalton's work inspired the great Swedish chemist Johan Berzelius who

Hydrogen	Strontium	Gold	H Hydrogen	Fe Iron
Azote	Barytes		C Carbon	Zn Zinc
Carbon	Iron	Silver	O Oxygen	Cu Copper
Oxygen	Zinc		P Phosphorus	Pb Lead
Phosphorus	Copper	Iron	S Sulphur	Ag Silver
Sulphur	Lead	Mercury	Mg Magnesium	Au Gold
Magnesia	Silver		Sr Strontium	Hg Mercury
Lime	Gold	Tin		
Soda	Platina			
Potash	Mercury	Copper		

Symbols for the elements used by (left) John Dalton, (centre) the early alchemists, and (right) Johan Berzelius. Modern scientists use Berzelius's system, which was adapted to show the exact composition of chemical compounds by the addition of numbers.

put the whole theory on a firm experimental basis. Between 1810 and 1820, he analysed over 2,000 inorganic compounds. He also gave us our modern chemical symbols, using the initial letter (or two letters where necessary) of each element's Latin name. In a compound, each symbol represented one atom and, where there was more than one, a figure was added. Thus H_2SO_4 tells us that sulphuric acid consists of two atoms of hydrogen, one of sulphur and four of oxygen. But Dalton's atomic theory gave no way of knowing how many atoms of each element occurred in the molecule of a compound. He himself gave the formula for water as HO instead of H_2O, and for ammonia as NH instead of NH_3. There was much confusion among chemists on this score for another 50 years.

Dalton was obsessed with the idea of the combination of different elements by *weight*. In 1808, the French chemist Joseph Gay-Lussac published the discovery that gases combine in simple proportions by *volume*. For example, two volumes of hydrogen and one volume of oxygen provide two volumes of steam. Three years later, the Italian Amedeo Avogadro adapted this law to the atomic theory by putting forward the hypothesis that equal volumes of all gases, at the same temperature and pressure, contain equal numbers of molecules. The word molecule is important here because his hypothesis distinguished between an atom and a molecule just as we do today. He suggested that oxygen and hydrogen, for instance, each consist of two atoms bound together, giving the molecules H_2 and O_2. Thus in the example of Gay-Lussac's law given above, $2H_2$ (2 volumes of hydrogen) $+O_2$ (1 volume of oxygen) $= 2H_2O$ (2 volumes of steam).

Avogadro's Law

It was not until 1860 that another Italian chemist, Sanislao Cannizzaro, published a pamphlet showing how Avogadro's hypothesis could be used to resolve the confusion about atomic weights and chemical formulae. All that was needed was to weigh all the compounds of an element that were gaseous and compare them with an equal volume of hydrogen. For instance, of three gaseous compounds of nitrogen, nitrous oxide is 44 times the weight of hydrogen, nitric oxide is 30 times, and ammonia seventeen times. By experimental analysis, the proportion by weight of nitrogen in each compound can be found. Nitrous oxide will be found to contain $\frac{28}{44}$ of nitrogen, nitric oxide $\frac{14}{30}$, and ammonia $\frac{14}{17}$. It can thus be assumed that the atomic weight of nitrogen is fourteen as compared with the unit weight of hydrogen and that nitrous oxide contains two atoms of nitrogen, giving the formula N_2O. Avogadro had died a year or two before his hypothesis was thus promoted into the important law that bears his name.

From the tabulation of the atoms of different elements in terms of their atomic weight and the analysis of compounds into their atomic formulae, the next step was the investigation of the atom itself. As early as the 1830s, the English chemist Michael Faraday had shown that compounds could be split by an electric current in the process known as electrolysis. Like a number of his contemporaries, he thought that electricity provided the force which combined elements into molecules. The discovery of the electrical forces within an atom was made through experiments in the conduction of electricity by low-pressure gases. In gases at ordinary atmospheric pressure, electricity can be conducted only in the form of a short spark. Conductivity over a distance, as in forked lightning, requires enormous voltages. If the pressure of the gas is reduced, say to a hundredth of atmospheric pressure, an electric current passing through gives off a luminous glow as in the discharge tubes used for modern lighting.

If the pressure is reduced to one hundred-thousandth of an atmosphere, the gas itself becomes dark and the glass of the tube gives off a faint green light. Anything placed in the tube will cast a shadow on the end farthest from the cathode, which is the metal electrode connected to the negative pole of the electrical supply. Invisible rays must be coming from the cathode. In 1876, the German physicist, Eugen Goldstein, gave them the name cathode rays.

X-Rays

In 1895, Wilhelm Konrad von Röntgen, professor of physics at Wurzburg in Germany, was experimenting with electrical discharges

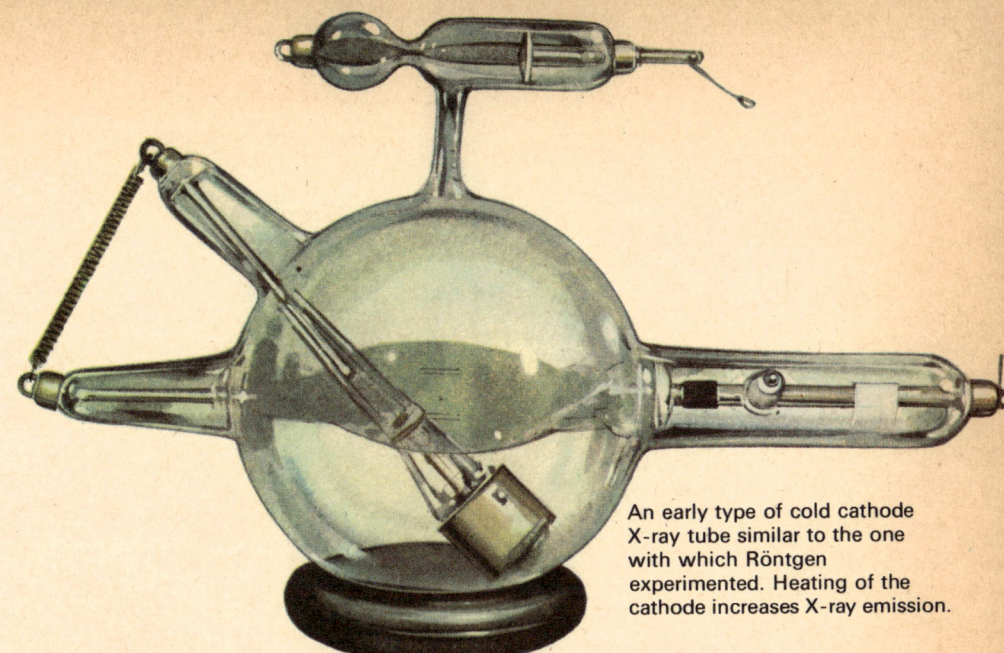

An early type of cold cathode X-ray tube similar to the one with which Röntgen experimented. Heating of the cathode increases X-ray emission.

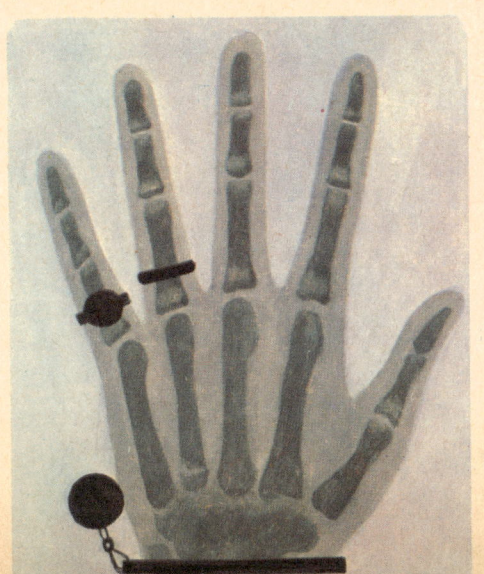

Röntgen (1843–1923), and an X-ray photograph of a hand showing rings and an identity disc.

Ernest Rutherford at work in the Cavendish laboratory, Cambridge, and a portrait of J. J. Thomson, who discovered the electron.

Apparatus used to break up nitrogen nuclei.

through low-pressure gases when he noticed a number of dramatic phenomena. A screen of barium platinocyanide fluoresced brightly when placed near the discharge tube. When he put his hand between the tube and the screen, a shadow of the bones of his hand appeared. Though wrapped in brown paper, photographic plates were fogged by the discharge. A key resting on a box of plates was reproduced when the plates were developed. Within a few weeks of the discovery, X-rays were being used in hospitals to examine broken bones and to trace objects swallowed by patients.

The nature of cathode rays and their importance in the discovery of atomic structure was explained mainly by the work of Joseph John Thomson (1856–1940) and his research team at the Cavendish laboratory in Cambridge. He discovered that X-rays caused a gas at ordinary atmospheric pressure to become a conductor of electricity. It was already known that positively and negatively charged particles, flowing in opposite directions, carry an electric current through a liquid. Such charged particles are called ions. It seemed that X-rays ionised the gas in a discharge tube. Thomson became convinced that cathode rays were streams of negatively-charged gaseous ions. When he measured their deflection in a magnetic field and saw the sharp outlines of the beam, he began to think that the particles were much lighter than atoms. Thomson performed a number of experiments to prove that the electrical charge on the individual particles of a cathode ray was equivalent to that of an ion in a liquid, but that the mass of the particle was very much less than that of a hydrogen atom.

A Model of the Atom

He had proved the existence of the electron. He showed that they could be produced not only in discharge tubes and by irradiating a gas with X-rays, but that they could be struck off a metal plate by ultra-violet radiation and were given off by incandescent metal filaments. They seemed to be part of all matter. Thomson put forward his model of the atom as a central positively-charged nucleus surrounded by rings or shells of electrons. He suggested that it was the outermost shell that gave an element its particular properties, irrespective of the total number of electrons it contained. Thus, elements with a complete outer shell were all chemically inert, those with one electron missing from the outer shell had similar chemical properties, as did those with two missing and so on.

Radium

In 1896, the French physicist Henry Bequerel decided to investigate whether all phosphorescent substances emit rays similar to X-rays. He discovered that salts of uranium affect a photographic plate. He put some uranium salt on an aluminium medallion on top of a photographic plate covered by an envelope and left them in a dark drawer for a number of days. When the plate was developed, there was an image of the medallion. The uranium obviously emitted a penetrating radiation. The phenomenon was to be named radioactivity by Marie Curie (1867–1934).

She was born in Warsaw and went to Paris to study science at the

Pierre and Marie Curie devoted their lives to the study of radioactivity.

Sorbonne. She met and married Pierre Curie, a teacher at the Paris school of Physics and Chemistry. She chose radioactivity as the subject for her doctoral thesis and went on to devote her life to it. She discovered that the ore of uranium, called pitchblende, is four times as radioactive as pure uranium. The ore must therefore contain some other unknown radioactive element. The Curies eventually analysed six tons of pitchblende from which they extracted only 0·1 of a gram of the new element which they called radium. They had provided the world with a treatment for cancer and, in 1902, were awarded the Nobel prize jointly with Becquerel.

Radioactivity

In 1897, a young New Zealander, Ernest (later Lord) Rutherford (1871–1937) began work on radioactivity at the Cavendish laboratory. He discovered three different types of radiation from uranium salt. The least penetrating one he called alpha-radiation, a more penetrating one which consisted of electrons he called beta-radiation, and the third, similar to X-rays and emitted during certain radioactive changes, gamma-radiation. Rutherford discovered that when radioactive atoms emit alpha-particles, which are charged helium atoms, their atomic weight is reduced and they change into a new family of lighter elements with different chemical properties. His assistants, Geiger and Marsden, bombarded a sheet of gold foil with alpha-particles and discovered that about one in ten thousand actually bounced back. From this, Rutherford developed his picture of the atom as a miniature solar system with orbiting electrons and a positively-charged nucleus which repulsed those alpha-particles that penetrated close to it. The work of another of Rutherford's assistants at Manchester University, H. G. Moseley, showed that each element in an ascending scale has an extra positive charge in the nucleus of its atom balancing its extra orbiting electron. Thus the lightest atom, hydrogen, has a nuclear charge of +1 and one orbiting electron, helium has a nuclear charge of +2 and two orbiting electrons, and so on to uranium with +92. The number of the positive charge is now called the element's atomic number. Gaps in the table discovered by Moseley were later filled by the discovery of the new elements hafnium (atomic number 72) and rhenium (atomic number 75). The particles representing individual positive charges within the nucleus were called protons.

Now the discovery had been made that the nucleus of an atom was itself made up of particles, Rutherford began experiments to see if protons could be knocked out of the nucleus of one element to transform it into another. He bombarded nitrogen with alpha-particles and noticed particles leaving the nitrogen with a longer range than the original alpha-particles. Nitrogen atoms had been disintegrated and converted into oxygen.

The Rutherford model of an atom has been superseded by the more elaborate models of today's scientists. However inadequate his description of atoms may seem today, in its time it gave rise to the nuclear reactor and the atomic bomb.

The English nuclear physicist Sir John Cockroft working in the Cavendish in 1932.

Theories of Light

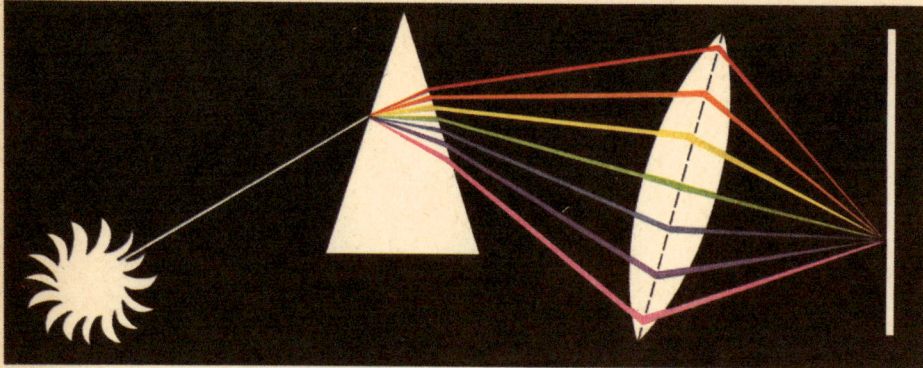

The composition of white light. The prism refracts the ray into a spectrum of different wavelengths, and the lens focuses them.

The problems of the transmission of light exercised some of the keenest analytical minds of the 18th and 19th centuries. The wave theory was perhaps founded by the Dutchman Christiaan Huygens (1629–95) who spent much of his life in Paris and had great success with his efforts to improve the telescope. He thought of light waves as the vibrations of the tiny spheres of matter comprising the 'aether', each vibrating sphere passing on the movement to its neighbour. He thought of such waves radiating from every point of a candle flame and crossing each other without interference. If light consisted of particles, he argued, they would be continually colliding with each other. Light to him was like sound waves. Sound cannot pass through a vacuum whereas light can.

Newton's Rings

In 1704, Isaac Newton published his *Opticks* which explained light as the movement of particles in straight lines. Reflection consisted of the bouncing of these particles from a surface. Refraction, or the bending of light, was due to their attraction towards the surface of a medium such as glass or water. If a lens is placed on a flat piece of glass, rainbow-coloured rings are seen round the point where lens and plate are in contact. Newton observed that rings of alternate blue and black were formed by blue light, alternate red and black by red light. The blue rings were about half the radii of the corresponding red rings. Newton supposed that the rings were due to the air between the two surfaces of glass being in some places prone to transmit light and other places to reflect it, and that this was caused by tremors or waves in the aether set up by the light particles striking it. In this case, Newton was suggesting a combination of particles and waves.

Thomas Young (1773–1829) examined Newton's idea that, if light consisted of waves, it would not travel in straight lines and sharp-edged shadows would be impossible. Young maintained that light wavelengths could be very short, that the spreading of light round corners would be very slight and therefore shadows would be sharp. He also introduced the theory of light interference which is the basis of modern wave theory. If two light waves are out of phase, that is if the crests of one wave-form coincide with the troughs of another, then they cancel each other out. This would account for the dark areas in Newton's rings.

Augustin Fresnel (1788–1827) in France showed that Newton's rings could be accounted for by the principle of interference. He further explained polarisation, which is the passing of a light through crystals in line with each other and the blocking of light when one crystal is opposed at right angles to the other. Fresnel suggested that light waves, rather than being to and fro pulsations in line with the direction of travel, were actually up and down vibrations at right angles to the direction of travel, like the waves in a length of rope that has one end moved steadily up and down. Such waves, operating in all directions, would be polarised into one direction as they passed through a crystal. Thus they would not pass through a second crystal set in opposition to that direction.

Modern light theory postulates waves similar to those of electromagnetic radiations and confined within the visible spectrum. But quantum theory also admits the possibility of particles found in the path of such a wave. The exact relationship between waves and particles is yet unknown.

Huygens believed that light was a wave form emanating from every particle of matter. The theories of Planck and Broglie show that neither he nor Newton was completely right.

Newton's disc and Newton's rings. When the disc is spun, the colours appear to merge and become white. Young was able to use Newton's rings to make the first accurate measurement of the wavelength of light.

Energy

The two concepts of the conservation and dissipation of energy apply to all its forms, but they were perceived and formulated largely through a study of heat. In the 17th century, heat was correctly thought to be the energy of movement of the particles of which a substance is formed. In the following century, this theory fell out of favour. The great French scientist, Lavoisier, thought of heat as a virtually weightless and indestructible fluid that could flow from one substance to another. He called this fluid caloric. After his death, his widow married the man who was to show that caloric could not exist. His name was Benjamin Thompson, Count Rumford (1753–1814). In a colourful career, Rumford fought for the Americans in the War of Independence, founded the Royal Institution in London, became minister of war to the Elector of Bavaria and a count of the Holy Roman Empire.

Noting how much heat was produced by the boring of cannon at the Munich military arsenal, in 1798 he set up an experiment in which a blunt steel bit was used to bore a brass cannon in a bath of water. After two and a half hours, the water boiled. The supply of heat from the experiment seemed inexhaustible. Rumford wrote that if heat could be produced in this manner and without limitation, then it could not be a material substance. He believed that only motion could have created the heat, which had not previously been present in either the cannon or the water.

Top: Rumford proved that heat could not be a material substance; centre: Joule proved that energy is always conserved; bottom: Clausius formulated the first two thermodynamic laws.

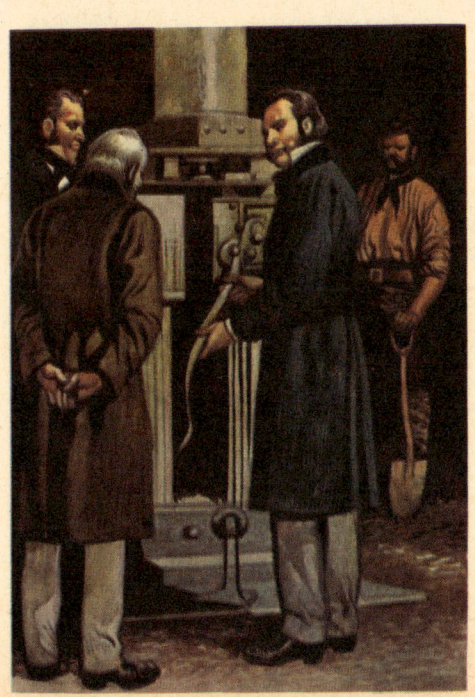

Lord Kelvin, as well as developing the science of thermodynamics, was a prolific inventor.

At the time, Rumford's findings made little impression on other scientists. About twenty years later, Nicolas Carnot (1796–1832), a French military engineer, began to study the steam engine with a view to improving its efficiency. He imagined an ideal engine working without friction and showed mathematically that the highest efficiency was obtained by the greatest drop of temperature between the hot, expanded gas and the cooled, condensed gas. He compared the fall from a high to a low temperature with the fall of water on a water-wheel from a high to a lower level.

Transformation of Energy

In England about 1837, James Prescott Joule (1818–89) began research to improve the recently invented electric motor. He realised that the source of electricity had to be cheap in relation to work done by the motor if it was to replace the steam engine. His experiments taught him that the loss of chemical energy from his batteries was equivalent to the heat generated in a circuit. He also noticed that when an electric motor was running it created a greater resistance to the flow of current than when it was at rest. The chemical energy from the battery required to overcome this increased resistance was equivalent to the mechanical work done by the motor. He was beginning to show the relationship between chemical energy, heat and mechanical energy. This led him to measure, with remarkable accuracy, the heat generated by mechanical work in such forms as the movement of pistons, the compression of air in a pump and the disturbance of water by paddle-wheels.

However, it was not Joule who first put forward the idea of the conservation of energy. This honour must be given to the German physicist Julius Robert Mayer (1814–78). On a journey to Java as ship's doctor between 1840 and 1841, he made the first draft of his

45

paper on the subject. He received little attention, and others began to express similar ideas. For Mayer, proving that the original idea had been conceived by him became an obsession. He was confined to an asylum and put in a straitjacket.

In 1847, Joule gave a lecture at Manchester which was a landmark in scientific history. He expressed his ideas on the conservation of energy—that energy cannot be either created or destroyed. He showed how energy can be transformed from one kind into another, that mechanical energy, heat, electrical energy and chemical energy are all equivalent to each other. He established Mayer's idea by the careful experiment which Mayer's studies had lacked. Joule's work aroused the interest of William Thomson, later Lord Kelvin (1824–1907), who had worked in Paris and was familiar with Carnot's theories. Thomson was attempting to reconcile Carnot's work with Joule's when Rudolf Clausius (1822–88) announced to the Berlin Academy of Sciences his two laws of thermodynamics. Thomson went on to develop the new science of thermodynamics, which is the study of heat in relation to other forms of energy, and to state Clausius's laws in clearer terms.

Albert Einstein (1879–1955) was exiled in 1933 by the Nazis. The remarkable tower shown here was built for him by the pre-Nazi government.

Thermodynamics

The first law of thermodynamics is that energy cannot be either created or destroyed and is the principle of the conservation of energy. The second law of thermodynamics is that heat, of itself, cannot pass from a colder to a warmer body. This second law cannot be proved and is what is known as a statistical law. The temperature of a body is made up of the *average* velocity of the molecules contained in it. Some molecules will be travelling faster than this average speed and some more slowly. When a cold gas or liquid is brought into contact with a warmer one, *some* of the molecules in the cold substance will be moving fast enough to pass into the warmer substance, but the *average* speed will favour movement from warm to cold so that the temperatures are eventually equalised. In other words, it is the very large numbers of moving molecules which make the second law of thermodynamics true in practice. Thomson went on to show that only part of the heat of an engine is converted into useful work, and that the remainder is dissipated into the air. Though the lost heat has not been annihilated, it cannot be recovered. Since all heat tends to pass from a higher level to a lower one, all the world's energy is tending to fall towards a uniform level. When that happens and no more energy is available for work, the earth will have become uninhabitable. Thus, the second law of thermodynamics embodies the principle of the dissipation of energy.

$E = mc^2$

Scientists in the 19th century had, of course, no idea of the vast amounts of energy locked up in the smallest quantities of matter. It was Albert Einstein, in the early years of our own century, who expressed this by linking the principle of the conservation of energy with that of the conservation of mass. He did this in his famous formula: $E=mc^2$. This means that the energy in ergs (E) is equal to the product of the mass in grams (m) and the square of the speed of light in centimetres per second (c). For example, a gram of any substance, if entirely converted into energy, would yield about 25 million kilowatt-hours.

Today, we believe that the sun's energy comes from annihilation of mass and that it loses about four million tons every second. This loss occurs during the transmutation of hydrogen into other elements. It can be calculated that a transmutation of a tenth of the sun's mass will take another 10,000 million years.

James Dewar demonstrates the liquefaction of hydrogen. In the course of his work he invented the Thermos flask.

Magnetism and Electricity

The phenomenon of magnetism was almost certainly known to man in the early Iron Age. Lodestone, the ore of iron known as magnetite, was used by the ancients as a direction finder. The ancient Greeks knew something of static electricity, as for instance, when amber is rubbed vigorously, it attracts particles of dust. Our modern word electricity is derived from *elektron*, the Greek word for amber. Benjamin Franklin, the American statesman, knew that like charges of electricity repelled each other and unlike charges attracted. He gave the two kinds of static electricity the names positive and negative to distinguish them. In 1752, he proved that a stormcloud was charged with static electricity when a kite flown into it drew a spark from a key tied to the lower end of the string. With this experiment, he invented the lightning conductor and proved himself one of the most foolhardy experimenters who ever lived.

Galvani and Volta

Luigi Galvani (1737–98), anatomy professor at Bologna University in Italy, first recorded the effects of electrostatic induction in 1780. He was dissecting a frog with a steel scalpel when an assistant produced a spark with a static-electricity machine. A momentarily induced current flowed through the scalpel, making the frog's legs twitch. Galvani tied the legs of a frog to a brass hook and hung it on an iron fence during a thunderstorm. He intended to prove that lightning would make the frog's legs twitch

Above: Luigi Galvani, the anatomist who first showed the connection between electricity and muscle movement. Right: Benjamin Franklin flies a kite to prove that thunderclouds are electrically charged.

The experiment which led Galvani to propose his theory of 'animal electricity'.

but found they did so whenever they touched the iron fence, whether there was any lightning or not. Galvani thought that the frog's legs contained what he called animal electricity. It was Alessandro Volta (1745–1827), professor of physics at Pavia University, who showed in 1800 what had really happened.

He demonstrated that the chemical action of moisture (contained in the frog's legs) and two dissimilar metals (like brass and iron) will generate an electric current. He went on to construct a pile of alternate silver and zinc discs separated by material soaked in salt solution, thus not only inventing the electric battery, but also producing the first man-made supply of electric current.

Still no connection had been made between magnetism and electricity. That was to be the great achievement of the 19th century, together with the means of transforming mechanical energy into electrical energy and vice versa. In 1807, the Danish scientist, Hans Christian Oersted (1777–1851), attempted to connect magnetism with electricity. He reasoned that the flow of an electric current through a wire should have a magnetic effect. To detect this, he placed a wire across and at right-angles to a compass needle, and then caused a current of electricity to flow through the wire. He expected the compass needle to line up with the wire, just as two bar magnets would tend to line up with opposite poles facing each other. Nothing happened. The compass needle did not move. It was not for another thirteen years that Oersted accidentally discovered that

Alessandro Volta demonstrates his 'voltaic pile' before Napoleon.

the compass needle had to be placed *in line* with the wire conductor to make it turn at *right angles* to it when a current flowed. At last, he had proved that an electric current did indeed set up a magnetic field, though not in the direction he had first supposed.

Magnetic Fields

A year later, the French physicist, André Marie Ampère (1755–1836), discovered that one electrical wire produced a magnetic effect in another electrical wire lying parallel to it. Two wires with currents flowing in the same direction attracted each other, while two wires with currents flowing in opposite directions repelled each other. Ampère had confirmed Oersted's finding that an electric current creates a magnetic field around itself. Could a magnetic field therefore create a flow of electricity? The discovery that it could was made in 1830 by Joseph Henry (1797–1878) in America, but at the time he did not publish it. The following year, the discovery was made again by somewhat different means and quite independently in London. The British scientist who did it and to whom can be credited the invention of the electric generator was Michael Faraday (1791–1867).

Faraday was the third child of a London blacksmith and received only the most basic education. He went to work as errand boy to a bookseller who later made him an apprentice bookbinder. He began to educate himself through his employer's wares. A customer at the shop took him to a lecture given by Sir Humphry Davy at the Royal Institution. Faraday wrote to Davy asking to join him in his research. It happened that a few days later Davy dismissed his laboratory assistant for misconduct. The job was offered to Faraday, who jumped at it. Within seven months, he was embarking on a journey through Western Europe as Davy's secretary and valet, during which he met most of the leading men of science. By 1821, Farday had made himself master of the study of electro-magnetism. In 1823, he was elected a Fellow of the Royal Society, and two years later replaced Davy as Director of the Royal Institution.

The First Generator

Three significant experiments of the many Faraday performed concern us here. On the 29th August 1831, he wound two coils of wire round opposite sides of an iron ring. One coil was connected to a loop of wire passing alongside a compass needle. The other coil was connected to a battery and switch. When the current was switched on in the one coil, it induced a current in the other coil which flowed only momentarily as shown by the deflection of the compass needle. When the current was switched off, again this induced current flowed momentarily. Faraday had discovered that induced currents were set up only by the *changes* of magnetism in the iron ring. On 17th October, he produced a current in a coil of wire by moving a bar magnet in and out of the coil. On 28th October, he rotated a copper disc between the poles of a large horse-shoe magnet. By means of sliding copper contacts, one at the rim of the disc, the other at the axle, he drew off the induced current to be measured by a galvanometer. The flow of current was continuous. He had created the first generator of electrical energy from mechanical energy.

All his working life, Faraday believed in the physical existence of lines of force of magnetism and electricity operating within the aether. James Clerk Maxwell (1831–79), who converted Faraday's experiments into the precise mathematical formulae they had lacked, believed in a similar theory. It was left to Heinrich Hertz (1857–94), professor of physics at Karlsruhe Polytechnic in Germany, to show that electro-magnetic waves are the same as light waves. In 1880, he produced electro-magnetic radiation, opening the way to radio broadcasting.

Michael Faraday at work in his laboratory. Faraday's discoveries explained the connection between magnetism and electricity and included the invention of the dynamo. They formed the basis for the modern electrical industry. He also formulated laws of electrolysis. Below: Faraday was a brilliant lecturer, and inaugurated the Christmas lectures for young people at the Royal Institution, of which he became director.

Organic Chemistry

By the end of the 18th century, mainly through the work of the Swedish chemist, Johan Jakob Berzelius (1779–1848), scientists were beginning to distinguish between inorganic and organic matter. The first was concerned with mineral or non-living materials such as water, gases, metals, salts, certain acids and oxides. These are composed of small molecules which can be broken up into their elements, joined in new compounds and returned to their original forms. Organic matter, products of the animal and vegetable world such as wood, sugars, fats and oils, remained a mystery. They burned or charred easily and could apparently never be returned to their original forms. Lavoisier attempted to analyse them by burning them in known quantities of oxygen and measuring the carbon dioxide (CO_2), hydrogen, nitrogen and water (H_2O) produced. From this it became known that organic matter was composed mainly of carbon, hydrogen, nitrogen and oxygen. At first it was thought that some living force gave combinations of these elements their peculiar properties. It was further discovered that two or more substances with entirely different chemical properties could have an identical composition of elements. Berzelius gave these different compounds of the same atoms the name isomers from the Greek for 'equal parts'.

Organic Compounds

In 1828, one of his former pupils, Friedrich Wöhler (1800–82), heated silver cyanate with ammonium chloride in solution to produce ammonium cyanate. When this was evaporated, he was left with clear crystals of urea, one of the constituents of human and animal urine. It was the first time that an organic compound had been created from chemicals that had not been derived from living matter. From that moment, the idea that a living force made some compounds different from others began to decline. The French chemist, Marcellin Berthelot (1827–1907), took the matter even further when he treated a number of alcohols in the glycerol family with acetic acid, producing entirely new fats unknown in nature.

Another French chemist, Jean-Baptiste Dumas (1800–84), made the discovery that the atoms of hydrogen

Liebig's laboratory at Giessen, where many of the groups of atoms known as 'radicals' in organic chemistry were first isolated.

in an organic compound could be replaced by chlorine, atom by atom, to produce a whole new series of compounds. For instance, the highly inflammable methane gas, CH_4, can have one atom of hydrogen replaced by chlorine to produce chloromethane, CH_3Cl, used as a refrigerant. The substitution of three chlorine atoms produces trichloromethane, $CHCl_3$, the anaesthetic chloroform; and the substitution of four chlorine atoms produces carbon tetrachloride, CCl_4, a chemical used in fire extinguishers. Dumas met so much hostility from his fellow scientists that he gave up chemistry in disgust and went into politics.

In Germany, Wöhler founded a school of chemistry at Göttingen University, while his lifelong friend, Justus von Liebig (1803–73), founded another at Giessen. They decided to conduct research together in an attempt to put some order into the vast number of organic compounds that existed in nature and could be created in the laboratory. Liebig had worked in the laboratory of Gay-Lussac in Paris. The latter had discovered that united carbon and nitrogen atoms could be transferred from compound to compound without themselves breaking apart. Liebig and Wöhler isolated many of the groups of atoms that behaved in this way, retaining their identity when combined with other atoms and acting like single atoms. These groups became known as radicals from the Latin for 'root', because from them more complicated molecules appeared to grow.

Combination of Atoms

An important step was taken in 1852 by one of Liebig's former pupils at Giessen, Edward Frankland (1825–99). He showed that atoms of certain

An industrial chemical works in 1865. Less than a century later the chemical industry had become indispensable as a supplier of raw materials for countless essential commodities.

elements combine with a fixed number of atoms of other elements. The combining capacity of an element or radical is now called its valency. Atoms with a valency of one, such as hydrogen or chlorine, combine with one univalent atom as in hydrochloric acid, HC_1. An element with a valency of two, such as oxygen, combines with two univalent atoms as in water, H_2O. An element like phosphorous has two valencies, three and five, and can produce two different compounds.

The man who brought all this into the pattern of organic chemistry that we recognise today was August Kekulé (1829–96) who had also been one of Liebig's students. Kekulé recognised the importance of valency. He established that carbon has a valency of four and that carbon atoms can link with each other. This is why modern organic chemistry is concerned principally with the compounds of carbon, rather than merely with the molecules of living matter. In the 1850s, Kekulé was working as a laboratory assistant at St Bartholomew's Hospital in London. On the top of a bus between Islington and Clapham, he fell into a daydream in which atoms dancing before his eyes suddenly formed themselves into chains. He tested the idea and found it worked. It can be illustrated by the series of hydrocarbons that begins with methane, ethane and propane, in which each heavier molecule includes an addition to the chain.

The chain pattern worked for the aliphatic compounds, so-called from the Greek word for 'fat', but not for another group called, because of their characteristic odours, the aromatics. It was found that the simplest aromatic compound, benzene, had six carbon atoms. This did not suggest a chain structure. Again, Kekulé had a dream, this time sitting by his own fireside. Again, the atoms danced before his eyes, forming into chains and then serpents. Finally, one snake gripped its own tail to form a ring, and Kekulé knew he had the answer. Kekulé linked the atoms of benzene in a ring with alternate single and double bonds to account for the four bonds of each carbon atom.

Synthetic Materials

Modern chemists have modified Kekulé's chains and rings to take into account the three-dimensional reality of molecules which limits the number of possible isomers. Yet from his models all the new materials in common use today have been built up. Beginning in 1856 with the first synthetic dye, chemists have created synthetic drugs, fibres such as rayon and nylon, plastics like bakelite and perspex, synthetic rubber, insecticides and weed killers, detergents, explosives, lubricants and fuels. It would seem only a matter of time before the organic chemist synthesises the highly complex molecules of enzymes, hormones and genes to create in the laboratory even the living cell itself.

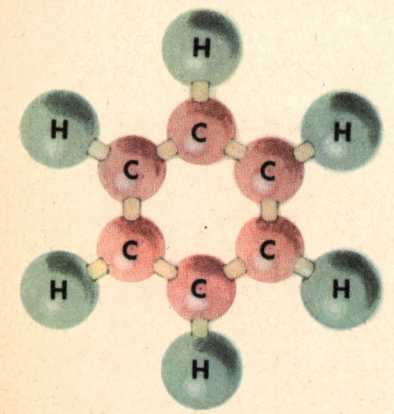

A benzene ring. Any or all of the hydrogens may be replaced by other radicals to form compounds including dyes and explosives.

Germs and Disease

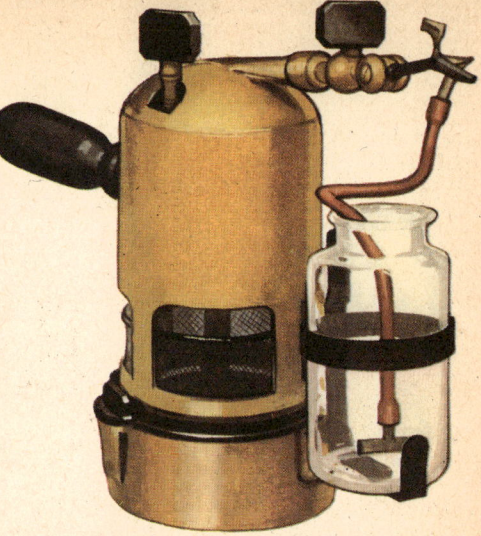

Left: Pasteur in his laboratory, where he exploded the myth of spontaneous generation of microbes. Right: Lister's carbolic acid spray.

Halfway through the 19th century, most of the medical profession thought that contagious diseases came from bad air, from a fatal miasma arising from decaying rubbish and the open sewers of cities. To combat epidemics of typhus, typhoid, dysentery and cholera, filth was cleared and laws passed to compel property-owners to provide proper drainage. To a certain extent it worked, since the places where microbes bred were cleaned up.

By the 1860s, it was becoming obvious that disease could be spread also by food and water, even from people's hands. A Hungarian doctor, Ignaz Semmelweis, had already reduced childbed fever in a Vienna maternity ward by insisting that attending physicians and midwives should wash their hands in chlorinated water. At the same time, the micro-organisms called bacteria were coming under the scrutiny of scientists such as Louis Pasteur (1822–95).

Louis Pasteur

A chemist with no medical training, Pasteur was asked to investigate the diseases that affect wines. His microscope showed him that, apart from the living yeasts that grow on the skins of grapes and cause healthy fermentation, there could be other micro-organisms. He became convinced that the latter were the reason for ill-flavoured wine. He tried antiseptics to destroy them, but found heat more effective, thus inventing the process later to be called pasteurisation. He also showed that micro-organisms were not spontaneously generated and indeed did not appear in truly sterile conditions. From this, he deduced that the diseases of both men and animals were spread by germs carried on dust particles in the air.

Vaccination against smallpox had been introduced into Europe by Edward Jenner (1749–1823). In 1796, he inoculated a small boy with matter from a cowpox sore on a milkmaid's hand. The boy contracted the relatively mild disease of cowpox. Inoculated with matter from a smallpox sufferer, he proved immune to the disease.

Pasteur tried the inoculation method as a preventive treatment against chicken cholera (no relation to human cholera). In broth, he made cultures of the microbes responsible and discovered that one such culture, several weeks old, gave chickens a mild form of the disease and thereafter immunity from fresh, more virulent cultures. Pasteur called his weakened culture a vaccine in honour of Jenner. In a similar treatment of anthrax, a deadly disease of sheep and cattle, he was forestalled by Robert Koch (1843–1910) who was to make Germany a world centre of medical science. It was Koch who, in 1882, isolated the tubercle bacillus, the first time a specific microbe was shown to produce a specific human disease.

Pasteur went on to cultivate the virus of rabies which he obtained in a weakened strain from the spinal cords of rabbits. He inoculated a nine-year-old boy, Joseph Meister, who had been bitten by a mad dog. Meister survived to become gatekeeper at the Pasteur Institute in Paris, founded to further the great man's work.

Antiseptics

Meanwhile in Britain, Joseph Lister (1827–1912) was applying Pasteur's principles to antiseptic surgery. By using a carbolic spray to kill germs in the air during an operation, Lister was able to use surgery in cases where the danger of blood poisoning, particularly hospital gangrene, had been previously too great. Nowadays, Lister's antiseptic methods of *destroying* germs have been replaced by aseptic surgery, the *exclusion* of germs from a sterilised operating theatre. Yet it was this great triumvirate of Pasteur, Koch and Lister who first put mankind on the winning side against disease by revealing the micro-organisms that are the true enemy.

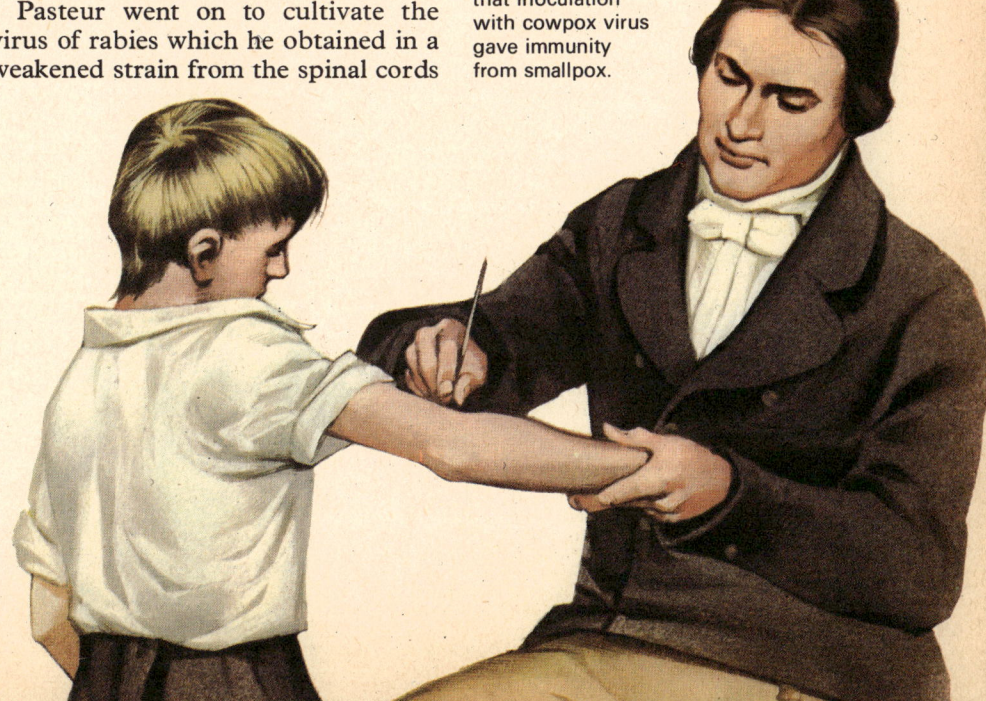

Jenner discovered that inoculation with cowpox virus gave immunity from smallpox.

A New Age of Invention

From its pioneer days, the steam engine did not alter fundamentally, though it greatly improved in efficiency, particularly in the ratio of weight to power. From Britain, railways spread to all parts of the world, and the United States became a centre of locomotive manufacture. Some improvements came from continental Europe. For instance, Marc Seguin, the French pioneer railway engineer, invented the multitubular boiler in which steam was raised more quickly by passing water through a network of heated pipes. Another French engineer, Henri Giffard, designed the first injectors which provided a means of introducing water into the boilers and avoided much of the delay in getting up steam again after an engine had been stationary for some time.

Inventors turned their attention to steam-powered road vehicles. The first of their kind had been built in France by N. J. Cugnot in 1769. It moved at a mere walking pace. In 1800, Trevithick had run his first steam carriage, and three years later demonstrated one in the streets of London. But it was not until 1831 that Sir Goldsworthy Gurney perfected a steam carriage, providing a regular passenger service between Gloucester and Cheltenham. The 14·5-kilometre (nine-mile) journey was completed in 45 minutes. Within three years, the first London steam bus was covering a 12·8-kilometre (eight-mile) route in under an hour on one sack of coke. In 1858, Thomas Rickett invented his road steamer which seated three behind the tiller and had a stoker standing on a platform at the back.

Steam Carriages
In France, Léon Serpollet invented a steam-generator with water pumped through coils of nickel-steel tubing which were made red-hot. He adapted this to a four-cylinder engine for a steam carriage produced from 1894. It became a familiar sight in both France and Britain. Meanwhile, in America the Stanley brothers had designed a two-cylinder engine for a wooden two-seater vehicle. Stanley steamers became very popular until they were swept into obsolescence by the model T Ford. Serpollet had been

Three steam vehicles, top to bottom: Bordino's steam carriage, 1854; Stanley's Steam Car, 1899; Trevithick's carriage, 1802. Early steam carriages were slow to raise steam and were charged punitive rates on toll roads: but the steam engine may still eventually replace the petrol engine on the roads of the future.

a manufacturer of steam tricycles which also enjoyed some popularity in the last two decades of the century.

Powerful railway interests were anxious to keep mechanical transport off the roads. For instance, in Britain in 1865 and again in 1878, acts were passed limiting such road vehicles to a speed of 6·4 kph (four mph) and insisting on a crew of two with a third man walking ahead to warn of their approach. It was thus the steam-traction engine that achieved the longest life. It had begun with the steam plough, a stationary engine used to pull a plough on the end of a cable. It was soon realised that it was more convenient to use a locomotive. The power of heavy-duty traction engines was much greater than the early petrol lorries. As a means of driving fairground machinery and adapted as steam-rollers for road building and repair, they remained in use into our own times.

The *Turbinia* at the Spithead Review, 1897. Development of the turbine was very rapid, although the basic design remained almost unchanged—the main difference being that modern turbines use steam at a very much higher temperature and pressure. Nuclear powered vessels use heat from the reactor to produce steam for the turbines.

Steamships

A more steady and lasting progress was made in the development of steamships. At the beginning of the 19th century, iron was already replacing wood as the material for sailing ships. By the end of the century, the steel steamship was queen of the oceans. In 1858, the *Great Eastern*, designed by Isambard Kingdom Brunel and the largest ship of the century, was launched. It combined iron construction, steam power and both paddle and screw propulsion. It was not a success, requiring much higher coal consumption than had been anticipated. Among early steel ships were those built by the Confederates in the American Civil War as fast blockade-runners. The great Cunard liners of 1893, *Campania* and *Lucania* had steam engines developing 30,000 hp, four times that of the *Great Eastern*.

By then, an entirely new prime mover had appeared, the steam turbine. The idea of steam-jet propulsion had been suggested by the Greek mathematician Hero as long ago as the 1st century A.D. Trevithick had produced a 'whirling engine' in 1814 which consisted essentially of two hollow arms mounted on a shaft. Steam escaped at a tangent from small holes at the end of each arm, whirling them round. The maximum of 250 rpm, however, represented only about a fifth of the potential power of the steam used.

Steam Turbines

The modern steam turbine was developed by the British engineer Charles Parsons who combined high efficiency with a high rate of rotation by passing the steam through a series of small turbines, dividing the fall of pressure as the steam expanded into a number of stages. Each turbine consisted of a fixed cylinder called the stator with stationary blades on the inner surface and a central rotor with similar blades. Steam passed through the stator parallel to the shaft and alternately between the two sets of blades, rotating the shaft. In 1884, the first steam turbine was used to generate electricity and ran at 18,000 rpm. Three years later, Parsons introduced a compound turbine with high and low pressure stages.

By the end of the century, his twin cylinder turbine was generating 2,000 kw for the German town of Elberfeld.

Parson's first attempt in 1894 to develop a steam turbine marine engine failed because the high rate of rotation could not provide the screw propeller with the necessary thrust. In 1896, he tried a system with three shafts each carrying three screws driven by a connected series of turbines. There was also a separate turbine driving the central shaft for reversing. Altogether, the engines of his ship, the *Turbinia*, developed 2,000 hp, and when she first appeared at the Jubilee Navy Review in 1897, she reached the unheard-of speed of $34\frac{1}{2}$ knots. Later systems included reduction gearing so that the engine could run at its most efficient and highest speed, while the screw propeller had reduced revolutions for maximum thrust.

Electricity

Early batteries suffered from a fall in voltage as the chemical products accumulated and the expensive copper plates were eroded. The first major improvement was the Leclanché cell of 1866, in which the electrodes were rods of carbon and zinc in a solution of ammonium chloride, materials used in the dry batteries that appeared towards the end of the century. The Daniell cell of 1836, in which electrodes were immersed in different electrolytes separated by a porous pot, was improved by J. C. Fuller in 1853. It gave a longer period of constant voltage and was used in the telegraph services into the 1870s. These were all primary cells with a limited life. In the 1860s, a Frenchman, R. D. G. Planté, developed a storage cell or accumulator based on electrodes in the form of large lead plates in sulphuric acid. It came into general use from 1880. During the charging period, lead peroxide formed on the plates. During discharge, the chemical reaction was reversed. A limitation to storage batteries was their weight, an accumulator for a simple lighting system often weighing as much as 113 kilograms (250 pounds).

Electric Generators

Immediately after Faraday had shown the way, mechanical generators of electricity began to appear, the first designed by Hippolyte Pixii and shown in Paris in 1832. It was turned by hand and had fixed coils with a rotating magnet. Rotating coils within a fixed magnet became general practice thereafter. These early generators provided alternating current, though a mechanical commutator to convert it into direct current was invented by Ampère and fitted to an early Pixii generator. Fluctuations of output voltage were evened out by the use of a combination of coils, called an armature, in which the maximum voltage was generated in each coil in turn. Electromagnets powered by battery had been known since 1825. Applied to generators, it was shown by C. F. Varley in 1866 that the electromagnet could be powered by diverting some of the generator's output and that sufficient residual magnetism was retained in the soft-iron core for the generator to be self-activating. In other words, a generator had only to be turned to produce continuous electricity.

When the steam engine was added to provide the motive power, the large-scale use of electricity was assured. In 1875, a generator was installed at the Gare du Nord in Paris to power

Thomas Edison with (left) an early carbon filament lamp and (right) Joseph Swan's lamp.

Electric street lighting in the City of London, 1881. The convenience and flexibility of electric lighting were quickly appreciated.

arc-lamps. In 1882, Edison's Pearl Street generating plant in New York was operating. In 1883, a small power station lit the Grosvenor Gallery in London and surplus electricity was sold to local customers. The power station designed by S. Z. Ferranti and built at Deptford in 1889 by the London Electricity Supply Corporation had four 10,000-hp steam engines driving 10,000-volt alternators and two 1,250-hp engines driving 5,000-volt alternators. It was the prototype of the modern power station. Ferranti invented a meter to measure customers' consumption. By 1886, work had been started on the first great hydroelectric installation at Niagara Falls using water turbines as the motive power.

Electric Railways

The principles of the electric generator and the electric motor are the same, the one working in reverse of the other. In 1873 in Vienna, Z. T. Gramme demonstrated two generators arranged so that either could be used to produce power to operate the other as a motor. These were direct current generators, and alternating current had become more common for large-scale generation. The first A.C. motor was invented in 1888 by Nikola Tesla and manufacture begun by Westinghouse of America. By the end of the century, machine-tool manufacturers were incorporating electric motors as an integral part of their machines, gradually doing away with the elaborate system of driving shafts, endless belts and pulleys that had been the factory's inheritance from water and steam power. In 1879, the first electric railway, 275 metres (300 yards) long and with current supplied to its three-hp engine by a central rail, was presented at an exhibition in Berlin. By 1884, Germany had the first electric trams with overhead power lines. In 1890, the first underground railway, the City and South London which passed under the River Thames, was operated by 150-hp electric locomotives.

Early electrical illumination was by arc lamp. As early as 1802, Humphry Davy had noted that a spark struck between two carbon electrodes gave a brilliant light. Yet it was not until 1857, when the steam-driven generator had appeared, that Frederick Holmes gave a demonstration of arc lighting suitable for lighthouses to the Brethren of Trinity House in London. Arc lamps were fitted into the South Foreland lighthouse in 1858 and four years later into Dungeness lighthouse.

Electric tramcars were a common sight in most large cities until they were made obsolete by the more manoeuvrable buses.

Electric locomotives made the building of underground railway systems possible.

Arc lamps lit by batteries had been originated in 1846 by W. E. Staite. One of his problems was that carbon electrodes burned away, increasing the gap between them and changing the intensity of the light. He overcame this with a mechanism driven by a falling weight which was controlled by the expansion of a copper rod as the heat from the arc increased with the length of the spark. In 1876, Paul Jablochkoff, a Russian engineer who had settled in Paris, devised a new arc lamp with the electrodes placed side by side vertically instead of end to end. The arc was struck across the tips which wore evenly as alternating current was supplied from a generator. A later improvement was to copperplate the carbon electrodes.

Incandescent Lamps

The incandescent filament lamp was developed simultaneously by Thomas Edison in America and Joseph Swan in Britain. Swan's lamp used a filament of carbonised, mercerised cotton, while Edison used a sliver of carbonised bamboo. Such filaments had a long life only if heated in the absence of air, so evacuated glass containers were necessary. Platinum wire was used to lead the current to the filament because it was the only metal available with the same expansion when heated as the glass. If the two materials had expanded at a different rate, cracking of the glass would have been inevitable and the vacuum impaired. Swan overcame the blackening of the bulb by deposits of carbon by removing the last traces of air with a 'flashing' of the filament just before the bulb was finally sealed. Blocked by a rivalry of patents, the two inventors formed the Edison and Swan United Electric Light Company.

Carbon filament lamps quickly replaced arc lamps for general use. In 1898, von Welsbach, who had pioneered the incandescent gas mantle, developed a lamp with a filament of osmium which has a melting point of 2,700°C. By the end of the century, tantalum with a melting point of 2,996°C was in use. Tungsten (melting point 3,410°C) became the common metal for electric light filaments from 1911.

Guglielmo Marconi (1874–1937) received the Nobel Prize for Physics in 1909 for his work in advancing wireless telegraphy.

The Telegraph, Telephone and Radio

The first practical use to which electricity was put was the sending of messages by telegraph. Early ideas involved the use of an electrostatic machine to charge wires which then agitated a pith ball at the receiving end. As early as 1753, a system had been proposed using 26 wires, one for each letter of the alphabet. Later schemes reduced the wires to one and used a code. The invention of the electric cell attracted the German inventor S. T. von Soemmering to devise a telegraph. He demonstrated it to an attaché at the Russian Legation in Munich, Baron Schilling, who attempted to develop it. The establishment of a connection between magnetism and electricity suggested to Schilling an electromagnetic receiver based on the movement of a single needle allied to a code. One of his instruments was seen by William Cooke who, on his return to London, went into partnership with Charles Wheatstone, professor of natural philosophy at King's College.

Cooke and Wheatstone patented their first five-needle telegraph in 1837. The following year, they designed a two-needle version to connect West Drayton with Paddington station on the Great Western Railway. Four years later, the telegraph was extended as far as Slough. In 1845, it attracted enormous publicity when a suspected murderer was seen boarding a London train at Slough and the information was telegraphed to Paddington where the police arrested him. This type of telegraph required a code, and the one that was adopted eventually throughout the world was the invention of Samuel Morse. He had the good fortune to establish the first telegraphic link between Washington and Baltimore the day before the Democratic Convention met to choose its presidential candidate, and the election result was the first important news transmitted by it. From such dramatic beginnings, the telegraph spread rapidly. A submarine cable linked Britain with the Continent in 1851. After considerable difficulties, a transatlantic cable was operating by 1866. In 1872, when the mayors of London and Adelaide, Australia exchanged messages, cables linked many cities.

As early as 1845, a method of printing the message was devised. Wheatstone patented his printing telegraph in 1860. Meanwhile, the German physicist, Hermann Helmholtz, was researching into the reproduction of sound. Though an electric telephone was demonstrated in Germany in 1861, the first practical device was invented by Alexander Graham Bell and patented in 1876. In both microphone and receiver, Bell used electromagnets with pivoted armatures attached to metal diaphragms. Variations in strength of current varied the magnetic pull on the armature, setting up vibrations in the diaphragm of the receiver which transmitted the sound waves through the air. Conversely, sound waves impinging on the microphone diaphragm produced fluctuations of induced current in the electromagnet for transmission along the wire.

Samuel Morse (1791–1872), whose code of telegraphic signals is still widely used today, with (above) a Wheatstone perforator, which prints out telegraphic signals on a paper tape, and (below) a morse key.

The *Great Eastern*, for 30 years the world's largest liner, was used to lay a transatlantic cable.

The Phonograph

In 1859, Leon Scott demonstrated his 'phonautograph' to the Royal Association in London, proving that sound was a form of energy. The phonautograph consisted of a funnel with a diaphragm at the end attached to a stiff bristle which rested on a revolving cylinder coated with lamp-black. When the diaphragm was vibrated by sound entering the funnel, the bristle drew corresponding patterns on the cylinder. Scott's great discovery was that similar sounds made similar patterns, though he could see no practical application of the fact. It was Thomas Edison who, in 1877, saw the possibility that a permanent imprint of the patterns could be cut in a cylinder in such a way that the process could be reversed and the sound waves played back. Edison used a cylinder covered in tinfoil. The cuts in it were made vertically on a 'hill and dale' principle. Later, Tainter and Bell substituted a wax-covered cylinder.

The modern record player owes its origin to Emile Berliner, a German emigrant working in Washington. He replaced Edison's cylinder with a flat disc in which the cuts were made from side to side in a spiral groove, in contrast to the variations in depth of the cuts in Edison's early machines. Thus he combined Edison's idea of a permanent imprint with Scott's 'writing in sound'. Edison adapted his phonograph to incorporate the advantage of Berliner's method of cutting, but it was eventually the flat disc, with its technical superiority, that prevailed. Berliner began by etching the recording on glass, but soon changed to zinc. By 1888, he had found a way of making a master from which copies could be taken. Recordings were made mechanically, directly from the sound waves, for many years. Electrical recording was not invented until 1925.

Meanwhile, an even more revolutionary method of electrical communication was slowly emerging throughout the 19th century. Faraday's work on electromagnetism had propagated the idea of lines of force along which magnetism and electricity acted. James Clerk Maxwell, who translated much of Faraday's theory into mathematical terms, put forward the idea that electrical disturbances through space resemble the transmission of light. It was left to the German physicist, Heinrich Hertz, to produce in the laboratory the electromagnetic waves that Maxwell's theories postulated. He showed that a flow of current in one circuit could induce a similar flow in another circuit not directly connected but tuned to the first. Hertz proved that the difference between electromagnetic waves linking the two circuits and waves of light was merely one of wavelength.

Radio Signals

In 1895, Ernest Rutherford used electromagnetic waves to transmit messages over a distance of 1·2 kilometres (three-quarters of a mile) at Cambridge. Even then it was not considered possible to transmit radio waves over a great distance because of the curvature of the earth's surface. It was thought the waves would just fly off into space. Then, on 12th December 1901, Guglielmo Marconi, an Italian engineer largely ignorant of the physics involved, transmitted a radio signal across the Atlantic. Though Marconi did not know it, his success had been made possible by the ionosphere reflecting back his signals to earth. It was left to others to discover the existence of the so-called heaviside layer in the upper atmosphere. Marconi had used transmissions in the 300 to 3,000 metres waveband. It was not until much later that short waves, such as the 24 cms used by Hertz in his laboratory experiments, were found to be most suitable for long-distance communication.

Edison with an early phonograph. In 1877 he recorded himself reciting 'Mary had a little lamb'.

Internal Combustion

Like many early motor cars, this 1892 Peugeot owes much of its design to horse-drawn carriages. The driver sits in the back seat with passengers facing him.

Fuel for the early stationary internal combustion engines was usually coal-gas, mixed with air. The first fully successful gas engine was designed by Nicholas Otto in Germany in the 1870s. It worked on what became known as the Otto cycle and was adopted for almost all but the lowest powered internal combustion engines after 1890. It is based on a piston and cylinder with intake and exhaust valves and consists of four strokes: 1, explosive mixture drawn into the cylinder; 2, mixture compressed by piston and ignited; 3, explosion forces piston back; 4, returning piston drives out exhaust gases, and the whole cycle starts again.

Meanwhile, another fuel, at first used for lighting and heating, was able to compete in price with coal-gas. This was petroleum, which had the enormous advantage of being easy to transport. A fairly heavy kerosene oil was at first used for internal combustion. This had to be either vaporised by heating or atomised into a fine spray and mixed with air to form the explosive material. It could then be spontaneously ignited by extreme compression. The name chiefly associated with the oil engine is Rudolf Diesel, a German engineer who was nearly killed when his first engine exploded, and who finally disappeared mysteriously from the Harwich steam ferry on his way to London. In 1897, his engine managed to achieve the high compression ratio required, though diesel engines need to be of robust and heavy construction, making them most useful for heavy land transport, marine and large stationary engines.

Daimler and Benz

Two Germans can be said to have developed the petrol engine for use with the lighter, more volatile fuel-oil. One of these was Gottlieb Daimler whose single cylinder vertical engine worked on the Otto cycle with fuel ignited by a heated tube in the cylinder head. By 1886, it had been fitted to a bicycle and a carriage. The other engineer was Karl Benz who made engines specifically for motor cars. His engine was horizontal and had electrical ignition supplied by an induction coil from an accumulator. This was fitted with a rotary contact breaker driven from the engine to ensure accurate timing for the spark which was produced in a plug essentially the same as the one used today. After 1893, the modern float-feed carburettor, invented by Wilhelm Maybach, came into general use. The float worked a needle valve. Suction from the cylinder drew petrol through a fine nozzle into the air intake.

The first petrol-powered vehicle with an engine mounted on a handcart is credited to an Austrian inventor, Siegfried Markus, and given the date 1864. Nothing came of it, however, and Benz is usually considered the pioneer

Gottlieb Daimler (1834–1900) first put the Otto engine to use.

Karl Benz (1844–1929) is credited with building the first motor car.

An 1897 Daimler with the front engine, rear wheel drive layout which soon became standard.

The development of the bicycle. Top: the machine which started it all—an early 19th-century dandy-horse, which the rider pushed along with his feet on the ground. Centre is a tandem tricycle, with two sets of pedals but no brakes. The tricycle was very stable, especially in comparison with its contemporary the penny-farthing. Bottom is a modern bicycle with brakes, gears, mudguards and pneumatic tyres. The picture (left) shows a late 19th-century bicycle club outing. The introduction of the pneumatic tyre at the end of the century brought about a tremendous upsurge of interest in the bicycle as a cheap and convenient means of transport. Although the advent of the mass-produced motor car reduced the demand, there is renewed interest in the bicycle now as cities become more congested and the costs of motoring continue to soar.

of the motor car. In 1885, he built a light vehicle with a single cylinder engine, a vertical crankshaft and a belt-drive which could be moved from a fixed to a loose pulley thus acting as a primitive kind of clutch so that the engine could idle in neutral. The vehicle had a single front wheel steered by a tiller. Within eight years, Benz had developed a four-wheeler with a horizontal crankshaft, a design which was being manufactured in hundreds by the end of the century.

Meanwhile, in 1886, Daimler was trying out his high-speed engine, the first of its kind, on a motorcycle. A year later, he fitted one to the rear end of an experimental carriage. His four-wheeled motor carriages, ancestors of the Mercédes cars, were produced at the famous Canstatt works near Stuttgart.

Early motor cars were made for the enthusiast and the well-to-do. In 1896, Henry Ford made his first car. In 1903, he founded the Ford Motor Company. By 1908, he had designed the Model T for mass production. In nineteen years without major design changes, it sold over fifteen million. The motoring age had dawned.

The Bicycle

Even after Ford and others had provided a cheap motor car, the bicycle remained a popular means of transport and, perhaps more particularly, an instrument of healthy exercise. Wheeled vehicles propelled by hand or foot go back to the 18th century. An early bicycle appeared in Paris about 1808 and an improved version of ten years later was designed by Baron von Drais at Mannheim in Germany. It was called the *draisin* or, more popularly, the dandy-horse. It consisted of two wheels running in the same track, joined by a wooden bar on which the saddle was mounted well forward. There was a rest for the forearms and a steering lever in front of that. The machine was propelled by the rider pushing each foot in turn against the ground. About 1840, cranks were fitted to the rear wheels with levers to operate them, by a Scottish blacksmith, Kirkpatrick Macmillan, who also thoughtfully added a brake.

A Frenchman, Pierre Michaux, first put cranks and pedals directly on the front wheel in the 1860s. He formed a company to manufacture his velocipedes. By the eighties there were more than 200 different kinds on the market, including tandems, bicycles with two parallel wheels, tricycles and even four-wheelers. The most common type was the penny-farthing on which the rider balanced rather dangerously above a front wheel that was made as large as possible so that the maximum distance would be travelled for each revolution of the pedals fixed directly to the wheel. The next step was the introduction in 1885 of a chain-drive geared to the rear wheel. This invention was known, understandably, as the safety bicycle and is credited to J. K. Starley of Coventry.

Early bicycles had steel tyres, from which some types were known popularly as boneshakers. The pneumatic tyre had been patented in 1845, but had to be reinvented by a Scottish veterinary surgeon, J. B. Dunlop, in 1886, to improve the comfort of his ten-year-old son's bicycle. There followed a boom in bicycle manufacture and many hastily formed companies going bankrupt. The bicycle had established itself as a firm favourite. It was the universal vehicle for the young, and initiated a vast array of touring clubs and sporting events.

Powered Flight

Lighter-than-air machines, such as balloons and airships, are dealt with elsewhere in this volume. Here, we are concerned with the heavier-than-air flying machines and the application of motive power to them. The ancient Chinese probably had kites big enough to carry a man, and they certainly had toy helicopters. Early ideas about human flight were based on the flight of birds and involved aircraft with flapping wings called ornithopters. Model ornithopters have actually flown, but none large enough to carry a human. Yet from the time around 1500 when Leonardo da Vinci began to take them seriously, much effort was expended on them.

The beginning of the modern aeroplane dates from the work of Sir George Cayley (1773–1857). He worked out the problems of aerodynamics and aerostatics and set about solving them by experiment. He kept records from which later inventors could follow his progress. He saw at once, unlike most of the other pioneers, that a fixed wing was essential. He made model gliders from 1804 and throughout the following 50 years, flying them from hilltops. He is believed to have been successful on two occasions in building and flying a glider over a short distance with a human pilot. His findings were published and encouraged others to attempt to solve the remaining problems of sustained and controlled flight.

Below: Otto Lilienthal in his 'hanging glider'. This type of gliding is now gaining popularity as a sport.

Man-carrying Gliders

Success with man-carrying gliders was eventually achieved by the German, Otto Lilienthal, and his English follower, P. S. Pilcher. During the early 1890s, Lilienthal made more than a thousand flights in his so-called hanging glider. Pilcher also flew towed gliders. Both men were killed in gliding accidents, Lilienthal in 1896 and Pilcher in 1899.

Meanwhile, from 1827, attempts were made to produce a man-carrying monoplane kite. Success was not achieved until L. Hargrave in Australia produced in 1893 a box kite with two fixed lifting surfaces. This design was being studied by Pilcher at the time of his death. A French engineer, Octave Chanute, also experimented with both the box kite and gliders. He passed his design for a trussed biplane structure to the Wright brothers and gave them encouragement in other ways. In 1848, a lacemaker from Chard, John Stringfellow, managed to fly a model fixed-wing aeroplane on the end of a wire, though it is believed that his design was fundamentally unsound. Others produced powered models that took off from the ground and used many different power sources, including rubber bands, clockwork, steam and compressed air. By 1866 when the (now Royal) Aeronautical Society was founded in Britain, most of the vital theories of aerodynamics had been published. There was even a dart-shaped design which it was suggested could be powered by a steam jet, anticipating by nearly 100 years modern ideas of rocket propulsion. The model aeroplane enthusiasm culminated in a design by an American professor of astronomy, S. P. Langley, whose 4·8-metre (sixteen foot) wingspan, steam-powered monoplane flew for a distance of 1·2 kilometres (three-quarters of a mile).

Powered Flight

By that time, the development of the petrol engine was beginning to show

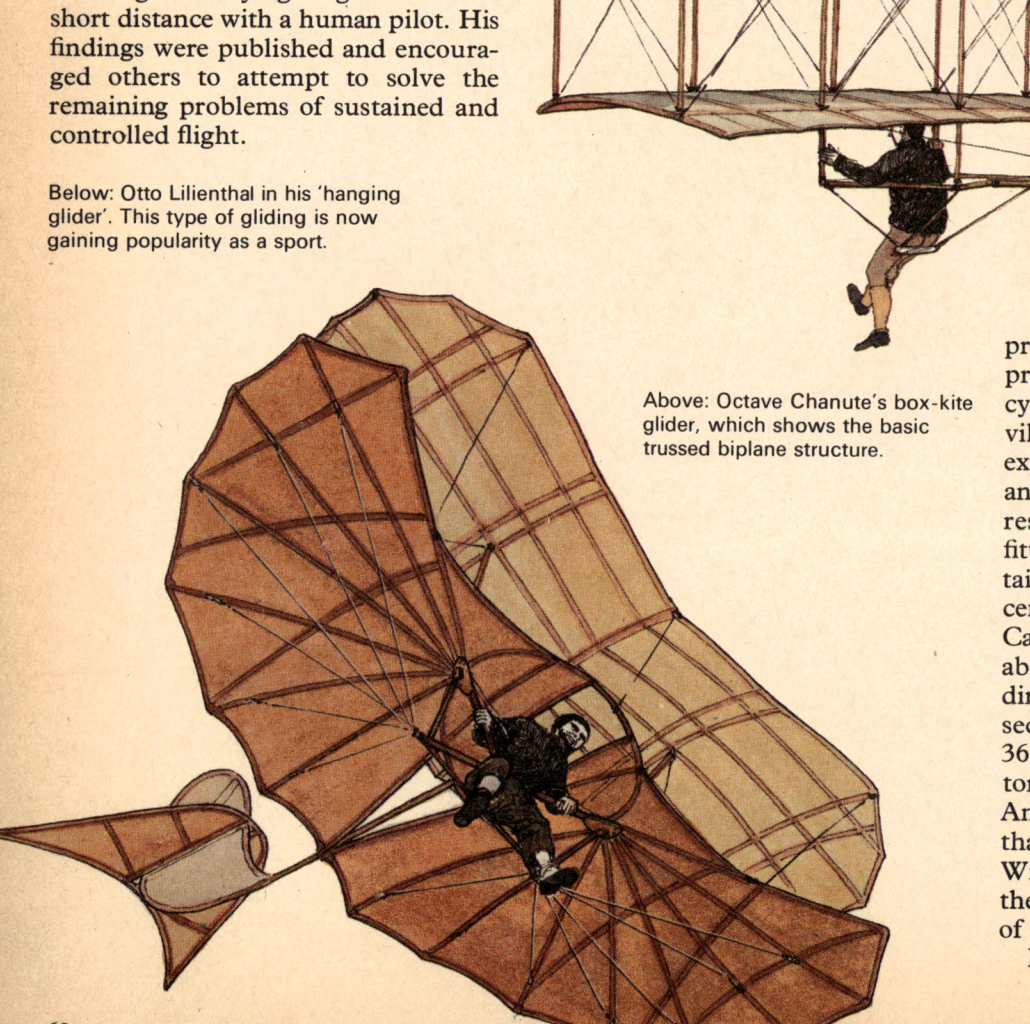

Above: Octave Chanute's box-kite glider, which shows the basic trussed biplane structure.

promise as the final solution to the problem of powered flight. Two bicycle manufacturers, the brothers Orville and Wilbur Wright, had been experimenting with gliders. They built and flew three in 1900, 1901 and 1902 respectively. At last, in 1903, they fitted a twelve hp petrol engine to a tailless pusher biplane. On 17th December near Kitty Hawk in North Carolina, Orville took it with reasonable control of height, speed and direction through its first twelve-second flight, covering a distance of 36·5 metres (40 yards). Yet this historic event was virtually ignored by the American press. It was not until 1908 that an improved version of the Wright's biplane flew in Europe, and the western world began to take note of their achievement.

Before that, in 1906, the Brazilian

A 'Wright Flyer' of 1908. The 'tail-first' construction was later abandoned, but the Wrights continued to use pusher propellers. Their main problem was the instability of their machine in flight.

Wilbur Wright

Orville Wright

Hubert Latham's *Antoinette*, one of Bleriot's rivals in the race across the Channel. In the event Latham's engine failed and he landed in the sea a few minutes after takeoff.
Far left is a poster advertising the first great aviation meeting at Rheims in 1909.

Alberto Santos-Dumont had made the first powered flight in Europe in his independently designed biplane which was, however, much inferior to the Wrights'. The Voisin brothers, in their factory in France, were building their box-kite biplane which formed the basis for many later double-winged aircraft. Louis Blériot was also at work on his monoplane. In 1909, he flew it across the English Channel. The publicity attending this event not only focused attention on the aeroplane as a possible weapon of war, but also established the monoplane design which was eventually to gain the supremacy. The biplane continued for a number of years because its wings were easier to brace. For speed, thin wing sections were usually used, though the designer Anton Fokker showed that a thick wing section could be used for cantilevered wings braced internally.

Aeroplane Design

The First World War gave a tremendous impetus to aeroplane design. Though their aerodynamic design did not make much progress, the power of petrol engines specially constructed for aircraft increased considerably. Already floats had been fitted in place of wheels so that aeroplanes could take off from water. Machine guns synchronised to fire between the blades of the rotating propeller were devised, as also were bomb and torpedo release mechanisms. When the war was over, efforts switched largely to passenger-carrying aircraft, and regular scheduled routes were opened up around the world. By 1930, the largest airliners had four engines and could carry 30 passengers at cruising speeds of 193 kph (120 mph). The flying boat was developed with a watertight hull and a planing surface along the bottom.

In the 1930s, the biplane of largely wooden construction gradually disappeared. Aircraft were built with a skeleton of light alloys covered by a stressed skin. Such airliners as the American DC-3 introduced refinements like wingflaps to increase lift for take-off and drag for landing, variable-pitch propellers, retractable undercarriage to reduce drag in flight and supercharged engines to increase speed at high altitudes. Safety devices were also included, such as radio contact with ground control, the radio compass, radio beams as landing guides and heaters to combat icing. Flying was set to take over long distance travel from other transport.

Index

(A page number in bold type indicates an illustration)

A
Abbé Ernst (1840–1905), 15
Accumulator, 54, 58
Acetic acid, 50
Acid, 21, 33, 34, 49, 50, 54
  See also separate entries
Aerodynamics and aerostatics, 60
After-damp, 19
Agriculture, 6–10
Air
  Experiment with, 20–1
Aircraft, 23, **23**, 60–1
Air-pump, 25
Airship, 22, 23, 27, 60
Alabaster, 13
Alloys, 39
Alternating current (AC), 54, 55
American Civil War, 10, 22, 53
Ammonium
  Cyanate, 50
  Nitrate, 34
Ampère, André Marie (1755–1836), 48, 54
Anaesthetic, 34, **34**
Aniline,
  Dye, 34
Animal breeding, 9
Anthrax, 51
Antiseptic, 34, 51
Antoinette, 61
Aqueduct, 10
Arc lamp, 54, 55
Argand, Aimé (1755–1803), 37
Aristotle (384–322 BC), 40
Arkwright, Richard (1732–92), 12, **12**, 13
Arlandes, Marquis d', 22
Asphalt, 29
Astbury, John, 14
Atmospheric engine, 24
  Pressure, 24, 25
Atom, 40–3
Atomic,
  Law, 41
  Theories, 40, 41
Avogadro, Amedeo (1766–1856), 41
Azote, 40

B
Bacteria, 51
Bakelite, 50
Bakewell, Robert (1725–95), 9
Balloons and ballooning, 22–3, 35, 60
Barge, 11
Barometer, 22
Baryte, **40**
Battery, 54
Becher, Johann Joachim (1635–82), 20
Becquerel, Henri (1852–1908), 42, 43
Bell, Alexander Graham (1847–1922), 56, 57
Benz, Karl (1844–1929), 58 **58**, 59
Benzene, **50**
Bergmann, T. O. (1735–84), 38
Berliner, Emile (1851–1929), 57
Berthelot, Marcelin (1827–1907), 50
Berthollet, Claude Louis (1748–1822), 34
Berzelius, Johan (1779–1848), 40–1, **40**, 49
Bessemer, Henry (1813–98), 38, **38**, 39
Best Friend of Charleston, **26**
Bicycle, 58, 59, **59**
  Tyre, 35, 59
Biplane, 60, 61
Bissell, G. H. (1821–84), 37

Bitumen, 29
Black, Joseph (1728–99), 21
Black-damp, 18
Blanchard, François (1753–1809), 22
Blast Furnace, 19
Blasting, 30
Bleaching, 33
Blériot, Louis (1872–1936), 61
Blood,
  Poisoning, 51
Boer War, 22
Boiler, 39, 52
Bone ash, 14
Bone china, 14
Bontemps, Georges, 15
Bord-and-pillar (mining), 18
Bordino, **52**
Boring-mill, 16, 26
Bottger, J. F. (1682–1719), 13
Bottle-making, 15
Boulton, Matthew (1728–1809), 32
Brake, *see* steam
Bramah, Joseph (1748–1814), 16
Brewing, 19
Bridges, 11, 17, 30, **30**, 31
Bridgwater, 3rd Duke of (1736–1803), 10
Brindley, James (1716–72), 10, **10**, 14
Broglie, Louis Victor (1922–), **44**
Brunel, Isambard Kingdom (1806–59), 53
Brunel, Marc (1769–1849), 16, 30

C
Cable,
  Submarine, 56
  Telegraphic, 56
  Transatlantic, 56, **56**
Campania, *see* Cunard liners
Canals, 6, 10, 28, 29, 30
Cancer, treatment of, 43
Cannizzaro, Stanislao (1826–1910), 41
Cantilever bridge, 30
Caoutchouc (india-rubber), 22 35
Carbolic acid, 34
  Spray, **51**
Carbon, 21, 38, **40**, 50
  Dioxide, 21
  Filament lamp, 54, 55
  Tetrachloride, 50
Carburettor, 58
Carnot, Nicolas (1796–1832), 45, 46
Carpets, 32
Carriage, 58
Cartwright, Edmund (1743–1823), 13, **13**
Cast-iron, 28, 39
  Bridge, 11
Cathode, 41, **41**
  Rays, 41, 42
Cattle, 9
Cavendish, Henry (1731–1810), 21, **21**
Cell (electric), 54, 55
Cellulose, 34
Cerium oxide, 37
Chanute, Octave (1832–1910), 60, **60**
Chapman, William, 28
Charcoal, **7**, 19, 21, 38
  Furnace, 38
Charles, Jacques (1746–1823), 22
Charles brothers (balloonists), **23**
Charlotte Dundas, 27
Chemical industry, 33–4
Chemical symbols, **40**, 41
Chemistry, 20–1, 49–50
Chicken cholera, 51
Child labour, **31**
Childbed fever, 51
China, 13, 14
Chlorine, 50
  In bleaching, 34
Chloroform, 50
Chloromethane, 50
Cholera, 51
Chromium, 39
  Steel, 39
Chronometer, 16, **17**
Civil engineering, 6, 10, 34

Clausius, Rudolf (1822–88), 45, 46
Clay, 9
  China, 13
  Kieselguhr, 34
  Pottery, 14
Clegg, Samuel, 36
Clermont, **27**
Clocks and clock making, 16
Clyde Ironworks, 19
Coal, 6, 18, 19
  Conveyor, 19
  Cutting, 19
  Gas, 36–7, 58
  Mines and mining, 6, **7**, 10, 18
  - Tar, 34, 35, 37
Cochrane, Thomas, 10th Earl of Dundonald (1715–1860), 30
Coke, **7**, 19
Coke, Thomas (1752–1842), **8**, 9
Colt, Samuel (1814–62), 31
Combine harvester, 10
Engine, *see* internal combustion
Theory of, 20, 21
Compounds, 49–50
Compressed-air brake, 29
Caisson, 30
Concrete, 29
Condenser, 26
Conservation of Energy, Law of, *see* thermodynamics
Cooke, William (1806–79), 56
Cookworthy, William (1705–80), 14
Copper, 40
  Mines, 6
  Plate, 54
Corn, 8, 9
Cort, Henry (1740–1800), 19
Cottage, 8
  Industry, 8, 12, 13
Cotton, 12
  Spinning, 12, 13
Cotton, William, 31
Cowpox, 51, **51**
Crompton, Samuel (1753–1827), 12, **13**
Crops, 8
  Rotation of, 8
Crystal, 15
Cugnot, Nicolas (1725–1804), **26**, 52
Cunard liners, 53
Current, electric, 57
  Alternating, 54, 55
  Direct, 55
Curie, Marie (1867–1934), 42–3, **43**
  Pierre (1859–1906), 43, **43**
Cylinder (in engines), 24, 25, 58

D
Daimler, Gottlieb (1834–1900), 58, **58**, 59
Dalton, John (1766–1844), 40 **40**, 41
Daniell cell (electrical), 54
Darby, Abraham, **7**, 11, 19
Davy, Sir Humphry (1778–1829), **18**, 48, 55
  Davy lamp, **18**, 19
Delft porcelain, 14
Derrick, 37
Detergents, 50
Deverill, Hooton, 31
Dewar, James (1842–1923), **46**
Diaphragm (in microphone and telephone), 56, 57
Diesel, Rudolf (1858–1913), 58
  Engine, 58
Direct current (DC), 55
Disease, 51
Dolomite, *see* magnesium carbonate
Dollond, John (1706–61), 14
Dounreay, **7**
Drainage, 29, 51
Drais, Baron von, 59
Dredging (canal), 11
Dresden pottery, 13
Drill, 30, 32
Dumas, Jean-Baptiste (1800–84), 50–1
Dunlop, J. B. (1840–1921), 35, **35**, 59
Dyes, 33, 34, 50
Dynamite, 30, 34
Dynamo, **48**

E
Eddystone lighthouse, 11
Edison, Thomas Alva (1847–1931), 54, **54**, 55, 57, **57**
Einstein, Albert (1879–1955), 46, **46**
Electric,
  Cell, 54, 55
  Generator, 48, 54–5
  Light, 29, **54**, 55
  Locomotive, **55**
  Motor, 45, 55
  Motor car, 58
  Railway, 55
  Tramcar, 55, **55**
Electricity, 6, 47–8, 53, 54–5, 56, 57
Electrodes, 41, 54, 55
Electrolysis, 41
Electrolyte, 54
Electromagnet, 54, 56, 57
Electron, 42, 43
Elements, 40
Enclosure (farming), 12
Energy, 45–6
Engineering, 6, 10, 31–2, 34
Engines, 58–9, 60, 61 *See also separate entries*
Entrepenant (balloon), 22
Epidemic, 51
Ericsson, John (1803–89), **26**
Ethane, 50
Ether (in medicine), 34
Evans, Oliver (1755–1819), 26 **32**
Exhibitions, 17
Explosives, 34, 50

F
Factory, 6, 8, 12–14, 15, 31, 33, 36
Faraday, Michael (1791–1867), 41, 48, **48**, 57
Farming, 8–10
Felspar (in pottery), 14
Ferranti, S. Z. (1864–1930), 55
Ferrous sulphate, 33
Fertiliser, artificial, 9, 34, 39
Fibres, 50
Filament, 55
Finley, James, 11
Firebricks, 38
Fire-damp, 18, 19, 36
First World War, 22
Flint, 14, 19
  Glass, 14, 15
Flintlock, 31
Flying boat, 61
Flying-shuttle, 8, **9**
Fokker, Antony (1890–1939), 61
Forage, 8
Ford, Henry (1863–1947), 59
Frankland, Edward (1825–99), 50
Franklin, Benjamin (1706–90), 47, **47**
Fraunhofer, Joseph von (1787–1826), 15
Frederick II (1712–86), King of Prussia, 8
French Revolution, 21, **21**, 33
Fresnel, Augustin (1788–1827), 44
  Theory of light, 44
Fulton, Robert (1765–1815), **27**
Furnace, 33, 38

G
Galleries (mines), 18
Galvani, Luigi (1737–98), 47, **47**
Galvanised iron, 39
Gambey, Henri, 16
Gamma radiation, 43
Garnerin, André (1769–1823), 22, **23**
Gas (coal), 21, 22, **22**, 41, 42
  Industry, 34
  Mantle, 55
Gas Light and Coke Company, 36
Gay-Lussac, Joseph (1778–1850), 41, 50
Geiger, Hans (1882–1945), 43
Generator, electric, 54–5
Genes, 50
Germs, 51
Geyser (gas), 36
Gifford, Henri (1825–82), 22, **27**, 52
Gilbert, J. H. (1817–1901), 34
Gilchrist, Percy (1851–1935), 38

Glass, 14–15, **15**, 33
Glider, 60, **60**
Goldstein, Eugen (1850–1930), 41
Goodyear, Charles (1800–60), 35
Gossage, William, 33
Gramme, Zenobe Théophile (1826–1901), 55
Great Britain (steamship), 27, 53
Great Eastern (steamship), 53, 56
Great Exhibition of 1851, 17
Green vitriol, 33
Guericke, Otto von (1602–86), 24
Guinand, P. L., 15
Guncotton, 34
Gunpowder, 34
Gurney, Sir Goldsworthy (1793–1875), 52

H
Hadfield, Sir Robert (1858–1940), 39
Hafnium, 43
Hancock, Thomas, 35
Hand-brake, 29
Harbour, 11
Hargrave, Lawrence (1850–1915), 60
Hargreaves (d. 1778), 12
Harrison, John (1693–1776), 16, **17**
Harvester, 31
Heat, 45–6, 58
Heathcoat, John (1738–1861), 31
Helicopter, 60
Helium, 23, 43
  Atom, 43
Helmholtz, Hermann von (1821–94), 56
Henry, Joseph (1797–1878), 48
Hero of Alexandria, 53
Herschell, Sir William (1738–1822), 15
Hertz, Heinrich (1857–94), 48, 57
Hofmann, August Wilhelm von (1818–92), 34
Holmes, Frederick, 55
Hormones, 50
Horrocks, William, 13
Horse, 9, 12, 28, 29
  In farming, 9, 10
  In mines, 28
  Transport, 29
Hosiery, 31
Howe, Elias (1819–67), 32
Huygens, Christiaan (1629–95) 44, **44**
Hydraulic press, 16
Hydrocarbons, 50
Hydrochloric acid, 33
Hydroelectric plant, 55
Hydrogen, 21, 22–3, **23**, 40, **40** 41, 49
  Atom, 43, 50–1

I
Ignition (electrical), 58
Incandescent lamp, 55
Industrial Revolution, 6, 12, 13, 24
Inoculation, 51
Insecticides, 50
Internal combustion engines, 6, 58–9
Ion, 42
Iron, 28, 31, **32**, 38
  Ore, 19
  Smelting, 6
  Works, 26, 28, 39
Isomer, 49

J
Jablochkoff, Paul (1847–94), 55
Jacquard, Joseph-Marie (1752–1834), 13, **13**, 31, 32
Jena glassworks, 15
Jenner, Edward (1749–1823), 51, **51**
Jet aircraft, 23
Joule, James Prescott (1818–89), 45, **45**, 46

K
Kay, John (1704–64), 8, **9**
Kekule, Friedrich August (1829–96), 50
Kelly, William (1811–88), 38
Kelvin, Lord, *see* Thomson, William
Kerosene, 37, 58

62